OVERCOMING CHALLENGES IN THE MENTAL CAPACITY ACT 2005

OVERCOMING CHALLENGES IN THE MENTAL CAPACITY ACT 2005

Practical Guidance for Working with Complex Issues

**CAMILLIA KONG and
ALEX RUCK KEENE**

Foreword by Professor Anselm Eldergill

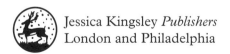
Jessica Kingsley *Publishers*
London and Philadelphia

First published in 2019
by Jessica Kingsley Publishers
73 Collier Street
London N1 9BE, UK
and
400 Market Street, Suite 400
Philadelphia, PA 19106, USA

www.jkp.com

Library of Congress Cataloging in Publication Data
A CIP catalog record for this book is available from the Library of Congress

British Library Cataloguing in Publication Data
A CIP catalogue record for this book is available from the British Library

ISBN 978 1 78592 259 6
eISBN 978 1 78450 548 6

Printed and bound in Great Britain

MIX
Paper from
responsible sources
FSC   FSC® C013056
www.fsc.org

Contents

Foreword

Professor Anselm Eldergill

This book is written by two leading thinkers in their respective fields so you would expect it to be very good. And it is.

Camillia Kong is a moral and political philosopher with interests in ethical issues around mental capacity and psychiatric treatment. Her previous book *Mental Capacity in Relationship: Decision-Making, Dialogue, and Autonomy* broke significant new ground in its exploration of the role of relationships in the decision-making capacity of people with impairments and mental disorders.

Alex Ruck Keene is well-known as a key British legal thinker in the field of mental capacity law. In recognition of his talents, both the Law Commission and the Department of Health have relied heavily on him in their development of new mental capacity and mental health laws concerning deprivation of liberty. As with many of the best legal thinkers, he studied the humanities (at Oxford and Johns Hopkins) before gravitating towards the law. That breadth of learning enables him to avoid the rigid and unimaginative tramlines that can limit the understanding of lawyers whose learning is limited to the law.

By combining the insights of a leading philosopher and lawyer, the authors seek to provide a set of ethical principles that can inform both the capacity assessment itself and the making of best interests decisions under the Mental Capacity Act. In pursuing that end they examine with great skill, clarity and empathy a considerable number of concepts and assumptions that underlie conventional professional approaches to mental capacity and incapacity.

Of particular significance is the concept of 'relational autonomy' and the role played in mental capacity by relationships—the fact that people 'are situated within complex relationships that can support and enable, as well as obstruct and disable their ability to decide, to act and to secure their own interests'.

This is not only relevant to determinations of whether a particular decision is in an incapacitated person's best interests. It also requires us to consider whether capacity is a narrow cognitive test or whether it is, at least in part, determined by the interaction between the person and their relationships. The authors believe that it is legitimate to interpret the Mental Capacity Act in the latter way. Furthermore, they consider that such an approach provides a better method of responding to the complexities of many cases. Everyone in the field can benefit from considering carefully their evidence and reasoning.

It is certainly true that one of the most difficult kinds of case in practice is that where a person with impaired mental capacity is living with a parent, spouse or partner in a relationship which professionals in positions of authority consider to be unhealthy. This may be because the professionals see the relationship as fundamentally abusive or because they believe it prevents the individual from developing independence. The professionals may decide to remove the individual from their home and their only close relationship in order to protect them from this harm, and to help them develop skills and potentialities which enhance their capacity to be autonomous.

The power of professionals to invoke what is called the High Court's inherent jurisdiction recognises that a vulnerable adult who is not incapacitated by mental disorder may be disabled from making a free choice because of the undue influence of a partner, family member or close friend. It must be true that a person with a significant mental health problem may similarly be vulnerable to undue influence, which in their case acts as an additional negative factor on their decision-making. However, it is usually difficult to demarcate the contribution made by the person's mental disorder to their active or passive decision to remain at home in the relationship, the contribution made by undue influence or unequal power, the interplay of these different forces, the effect of household relationships with professionals in positions of authority, and how the professionals' own relationships, past and present, colour their approach.

These are all profoundly difficult questions because there is no greater example of the undue influence of a third party on a person's life than the unjustified intervention of a judge, social worker or other professional in a position of authority. HL Menken once wryly observed that there is always an easy solution to every human problem: one which is neat, plausible, and wrong. Fortunately, the authors' approach is elegant and nuanced, and they resist the temptation to come up with simple, binary, answers to such complicated problems.

They remain throughout fully aware of the considerable dangers implicit in the concept of 'positive liberty' and any notion that autonomy requires a choice that is 'authentically' mine. Rather than honestly say, 'I know you don't think or will this but I sincerely believe that it is in your best interests', the authentic voice approach involves the professional saying, 'You may think you know what you wish but you lack reason and you are unable to exert your will. I actually know what you will, what you wish, better than you. The rational you wishes me to do this, to compel you to have this treatment that you appear to resent.' It is an approach that brings to mind the warning of Sir Isaiah Berlin:

> 'Even though men suffer ... in the process, they are lifted by it to a height to which they could never have risen without my coercive – but creative – violation of their lives. This is the argument used by every dictator, inquisitor, and bully who seeks some moral, and even aesthetic, justification for his conduct. I must do for men (or with them) what they cannot do for themselves, and I cannot ask their permission or consent, because they are in no condition to know what is best for them.'[1]

---

1   Berlin, Sir I, *supra*.

This is a powerful book which deserves a wide circulation, and not merely because it is elegantly argued and full of valuable insights. It is within the home and our relationships — not within Parliament or political assemblies — that the struggle for human rights begins, as Eleanor Roosevelt (the first Chairperson of the United Nations Commission on Human Rights) so eloquently observed:

> 'Where, after all, do universal human rights begin? In small places, close to home — so close and so small that they cannot be seen on any maps of the world. Yet they are the world of the individual person; the neighborhood he lives in; the school or college he attends; the factory, farm, or office where he works. Such are the places where every man, woman, and child seeks equal justice, equal opportunity, equal dignity without discrimination. Unless these rights have meaning there, they have little meaning anywhere. Without concerted citizen action to uphold them close to home, we shall look in vain for progress in the larger world.'

This book succeeds admirably in fulfilling its purpose of providing practical, reflective guidance to practitioners on various complexities within mental capacity practice, and in doing so makes a considerable contribution to the human rights of people whose lives and human rights are affected by such decisions.

Professor Anselm Eldergill

Chapter 1

The Legal Landscape and the Challenge for Practitioners

Introduction

Consider the following:

> Margo is a 68-year-old woman who is in the early stages of Alzheimer's. She gets confused periodically, but most of the time her memory is moderately good. She lives with her adult son who refuses to let social workers see her, although they were alerted to Margo's case after a concerned neighbour contacted the local authority. The very few times social workers have been able to see Margo, her squalid living conditions were thought to be contributing to her poor health: the house was extremely dirty with evidence of a rat infestation and she appeared to be not eating regular meals, with her weight dropping to dangerously low levels. In addition, her son exercised a worrying control over her. For instance, the fridge and pantry doors had locks attached, and Margo's son had the only keys. When asked about this, her son explained this was a necessary measure to prevent Margo from overeating. It is clear to the social workers that Margo's health and well-being are at risk in this situation – not only does her physical health seem to be suffering but also her Alzheimer's seems to be getting rapidly worse. Social workers think that both of these can, at least in part, be attributed to the son's power and influence in the house and the emotional distress that he causes her. Margo is adamant, however, that she wants to remain at home with her son. The social workers have to assess whether Margo has

capacity to decide about her living and care arrangements and if not, whether it is in her best interests to move her to a care facility and prevent contact with her son.

If you were the social worker, what would you do? What initial values and considerations would inform your decision? In the past, practitioners may have intuitively felt an obligation to intervene in situations like these, regardless of the paternalistic overtones. But in recent years our concept of mental capacity has altered the presumption towards paternalistic action, with the Mental Capacity Act 2005 in England and Wales (MCA) transforming the way in which practitioners in social care, medicine and the law are legally obliged to approach the decision-making capacities of individuals with impairments. The presumption of capacity in the first instance indicates an autonomy-based rather than paternalistic approach to deciding questions about a person's care and treatment. Within this framework, however, the appropriate course of action to take in Margo's case is not immediately clear – if she has the capacity to decide to remain at home and in contact with her son, does this mean practitioners do nothing? Equally, if she lacks capacity, does this mean practitioners ignore her deeply held values, which might include a relationship with her son and living in her own home? This dual impulse to respect the choices of individuals while protecting and safeguarding them from harm remains a fundamental tension at the heart of many dilemmas facing practitioners.

This tension is easy to state. Ten years of experience of the MCA in action has also made clear that it is impossible to pretend that individuals exist in isolation. Rather, they are situated within complex relationships that can support and enable, as well as obstruct and disable, their ability to decide, to act and to secure their own interests.

However, to date, what is all too often lacking is a clear framework within which to resolve this tension and answer these questions. By challenging the UK to abolish 'substituted' decision-making in favour of supported decision-making, the Committee on the Rights of Persons of Disabilities has made the tension even more acute, but without, on a proper analysis, assisting us to resolve it.

By drawing together the insights of a philosopher and a practising barrister, we seek in this book to provide a set of ethical principles that can inform and guide both the assessment of capacity and the making of best interests decisions under the MCA. These principles, we suggest, can help answer the questions of when and how professionals can intervene in a person's life to secure her greater autonomy, while respecting her as an individual – as a subject, not an object. In so doing, we suggest that we can start to bring home – to operationalise – the Convention on the Rights of Persons with Disabilities (CRPD) even without changes to the law.

Our key message is that we cannot properly deploy the MCA without a set of ethical *skills*. To that end, and in the body of the book, we aim to guide practitioners through ethical reflection in three key areas:

1. *The role of relationships in mental capacity:* why and how relationships matter in developing capacity and establishing supportive decision-making mechanisms; the defining features of those relationships that promote or diminish autonomy.

2. *The dialogical skills which enable and empower individuals with impairments:* what these dialogical skills are and how to cultivate them; the importance of critical awareness and understanding of how prejudices can impact on dialogue; how dialogue reveals aspects of capacity that may not be fully captured in the functional test and can impact on the outcome of capacity adjudication; reasons why an individual's participation is important in both capacity and best interests assessments.

3. *The role of the capacity and best interests assessor:* how social care workers, clinicians and legal practitioners can impact positively or negatively on the autonomy and agency of

individuals; how values inform and orientate capacity assessments; the need for transparency in capacity and best interests adjudications.

This chapter places what is to come later in the book in its context, providing an overview of the MCA, the inherent jurisdiction of the High Court, and the CRPD. We also explore the question of whether capacity is 'in one's head' or whether it is – at least in part – a function of the interaction between the person and her relationships. While some case law suggests the former, we ultimately suggest that it is both possible and legitimate to interpret the MCA in the latter fashion, and that this provides a better method of responding to the complexities of cases such as Margo's. This analysis provides the necessary framework for our discussions in the remainder of the book insofar as they relate to capacity.

Outline of the MCA, the inherent jurisdiction of the High Court, and the CRPD

The MCA was intended to establish a comprehensive statutory framework setting out how decisions should be made by and on behalf of adults whose mental capacity to make specific decisions is in doubt. It also clarifies what actions can be taken by others involved in the care or medical treatment of people lacking capacity to consent. The framework provides a hierarchy of processes, extending from informal day-to-day care and treatment, to decision-making requiring formal powers and ultimately to court decisions and judgments. The full range of processes was intended to govern the circumstances in which necessary acts of caring can be carried out, as well as the necessary decisions taken on behalf of those lacking capacity to consent to such acts or to make their own decisions.

Unusually for English legislation, the MCA is expressly based on statutory principles. Section 1 of the Act starts with three 'screening' principles concerning capacity: a presumption of capacity, a requirement to provide all practicable assistance before a person is treated as incapable and a declaration that a person must not be treated as incapable 'merely because he makes an unwise decision'. As regards the basis for acting or deciding on behalf of a person lacking decision-making capacity, the MCA is predicated on two overarching principles: (1) *best interests*: an action done or a decision made under the act for or on behalf of a person who lacks capacity must be done, or made, in his best interests and (2) *the least restrictive option*: before the act is done or the decision is made, regard must be had to whether the purpose for which it is needed can be as effectively achieved in a way that is less restrictive of the person's rights and freedom of action.

Section 2 of the MCA sets out the definition of a person who lacks capacity. Section 3 sets out the test for assessing whether a person is unable to make a decision and therefore lacks capacity. By applying these together, MCA 2005 adopts a functional approach to defining capacity, requiring capacity to be assessed in relation to each particular decision at the time the decision needs to be made, and not the person's ability to make decisions generally. Further, the inability to make the particular decision in question must be because of 'an impairment of, or a disturbance in the functioning of, the mind or brain.' Precisely how we are to interpret the words 'because of' is addressed in greater detail below.

Section 4, in turn, sets out a checklist of factors that must be considered in deciding what is in a person's best interests, aimed at identifying those issues most relevant to the individual who lacks capacity (as opposed to the decision-maker or any other persons). Although the test is intended to be an objective one, the courts have made clear that the purpose of the best interests is to require the decision-maker to consider matters from the person's point of view (*Aintree University Hospitals NHS Foundation Trust v James* [2013] UKSC 67). The person's ascertainable wishes and feelings therefore carry great weight, even if they are not determinative (*Briggs v Briggs & Ors* [2016] EWCOP 53).

Standing alongside the MCA is the inherent jurisdiction of the High Court to protect 'vulnerable adults': those who have mental capacity applying the MCA test, but who are or are reasonably believed to be, either (1) under constraint or (2) subject to coercion or undue influence or (3) for some other reason deprived of the capacity to make the relevant decision, or disabled from making a free choice, or incapacitated or disabled from giving or expressing a real and genuine consent (*A Local Authority v (1) MA (2) NA and (3) SA* [2005] EWHC 2942; endorsed in *DL v A Local Authority and Others* [2012] EWCA Civ 253). The precise extent of the High Court's jurisdiction – described in *DL v A Local Authority and Others* as 'the great safety net' – is unclear. In particular, it is ambiguous as to whether it is limited to taking steps directed against those who are coercing or placing the individual under duress, or whether the High Court can take steps directed against the vulnerable adult herself (i.e., to remove her from the place where she is subject to coercion).

As discussed in Chapter 6, we take the view that, while there is undoubtedly an important place for the use of the inherent jurisdiction to create a 'safe space' around the individual, its use against the person herself is difficult to reconcile with the distinction currently drawn in the law between those with capacity and those without capacity. There are other ways in which to draw the line, but for better or worse, the law at present in England and Wales does draw this distinction. One of the key purposes of this book is to outline how we can better respond within the framework of the MCA to those situations in which a person is suffering harm as a result of a *combination* of a cognitive impairment and the actions of those around them. We address this in the second section of this chapter after we have sketched an outline of how the CRPD challenges both law and practice in this area.

The CRPD was concluded in 2006. It seeks to bring about a radical change in the approach adopted in the social, political and legal arenas to those with disabilities (and, indeed, to the very concept of disability). Among other provisions, it seeks to bring about a fundamental shift away from the taking of decisions on behalf of individuals on the basis of an asserted lack of mental capacity. The CRPD has been very widely ratified, including by the UK. The CRPD has not been incorporated into domestic law, so it does not directly bind practitioners in the same way as does the European Convention on Human Rights (ECHR). However, it imposes obligations on the UK as a state, and is now routinely referred to by both the European Court of Human Rights and the English courts to help interpret the 'living instrument' of the ECHR as it applies to person with disabilities. At least as interpreted by the Committee on the Rights of Persons with Disabilities, compliance with Article 12 of the CRPD (which provides for equal recognition before the law) means that states party to the CRPD should replace legislation providing for substitute decision-making for incapacitated adults based 'on what is believed to be in the objective "best interests" of the person concerned, as opposed to being based on the person's own will and preferences'.[1] The Committee also denies the validity of the concept of mental capacity, contending that it is contingent on social and political contexts 'as are the disciplines, professions and practices which play a dominant role in assessing mental capacity.'[2] In 2017, the Committee examined the compliance of the UK with the CRPD, and recommended that the UK 'abolish[ed] all forms of substituted decision-making concerning all spheres and areas of life by reviewing and adopting new legislation in accordance with the Convention to initiate new policies in both mental capacity and mental health laws,' and 'repeal[ed] legislation and practices that authorise non-consensual involuntary, compulsory treatment and detention of persons with disabilities on the basis of actual or perceived impairment'.[3] Adopting this recommendation would mean repealing not just the Mental Health Act 1983 but also the MCA. There is, in reality, little prospect that the government will do so; further, there is a live and hot debate as to whether the government *should* do so.

---

1   Committee on the Rights of Persons with Disabilities, 'General Comment on Article 12: Equal recognition before the law,' para 23. Available at: www.ohchr.org/EN/HRBodies/CRPD/Pages/GC.aspx.
2   Ibid, para 14.
3   Concluding Observations on the United Kingdom (3 October 2017, CRPD/C/GBR/CO/1), paras 31 and 35.

That debate is outside the scope of this book.[4] Our core task is to enable those applying the law *as it stands* to better respond to situations of complexity, rather to suggest how the law might change.[5] Nonetheless, we should perhaps lay our cards on the table here and make clear that:

- We do not consider the concept of mental capacity to be fundamentally illegitimate, even if we would be the first to admit that *how* it is assessed often leaves much to be desired.

- We do not consider the concept of 'best interests' to be fundamentally illegitimate, especially where it is interpreted in the fashion required by the case law, which requires real weight to be given to the wishes and feelings of the individual.

- As discussed further in Chapter 2, we consider that the approach of the Committee on the Rights of Persons with Disabilities is predicated on an extremely 'thin' version of autonomy which does not always serve the interests of individuals with cognitive impairments.

- Intervention to secure the interests of those with cognitive impairments enmeshed in disabling relationships is not contrary to the CRPD (taken as a whole) and in fact can be *required*, by Article 16(1).[6] Such interventions should – primarily – be directed against the third parties who are harming the interests of the individual. However, steps can properly be taken in the best interests of the individual

---

4   It is covered, for instance, in the report of the Essex Autonomy Project on compliance of the mental capacity regimes in the UK with the CRPD: https://autonomy.essex.ac.uk/subject/crpd.

5   However, one of us (ARK) has been heavily involved in law reform work in this area as consultant to the Law Commission's Mental Capacity and Deprivation of Liberty project (Law Com No 272 (Law Commission 2017)).

6   Article 16(1) requires States Parties to 'take all appropriate legislative, administrative, social, educational and other measures to protect persons with disabilities, both within and outside the home, from all forms of exploitation, violence and abuse, including their gender-based aspects'.

where she lacks the requisite mental capacity (i.e., to remove her to a safe place or prevent her having contact with the abuser) and where such steps can properly be justified as promoting her health, welfare, self-respect and dignity – for instance, her autonomy in the wider sense.[7] This is so even if the individual objects to those steps. However, the greater the objection, the greater the justification required.

• While it is not the primary focus of this book, there may also be circumstances when, so as to secure these same interests, care or treatment may need to be delivered to an individual lacking capacity to consent. Again, such may be done in the face of her objection where there are sufficiently cogent reasons to consider that such will secure her health, welfare, self-respect and dignity.

Capacity: causative nexus or embedded within actual circumstances?

As set out above, we share the view that the concept of mental capacity is legitimate; further, we share the aim that we want to write a book which is of use to practitioners applying the MCA as it stands. However, we also share grave reservations about one model of decision-making capacity which entirely divorces the individual's cognitive abilities from the circumstances in which she finds herself. As we have seen above, the MCA provides that a person lacks capacity in relation to a matter if at the material time, she is unable to make a decision in relation to it (i.e., she cannot understand, retain, use or weigh the relevant information, or communicate her decision) *because of* a disturbance or impairment in the functioning of her mind or brain. As MacFarlane LJ put it in *PC & NC v City of York Council* [2013] EWCA Civ 478, 'for the

---

7   Article 16(4) provides that 'States Parties shall take all appropriate measures to promote the physical, cognitive and psychological recovery, rehabilitation and social reintegration of persons with disabilities who become victims of any form of exploitation, violence or abuse, including through the provision of protection services.'

Court to have jurisdiction to make a best interests determination, the statute requires there to be a clear *causative nexus* between mental impairment and any lack of capacity that may be found to exist'(para. 52, emphasis added). This was amplified by Parker J in *NCC v TB and PB* [2014] EWCOP 14. Interpreting what MacFarlane LJ had said in *York*, Parker J held that 'the true question is whether the impairment/disturbance of mind is an effective, material or operative cause. Does it cause the incapacity, even if other factors come into play? This is a purposive construction' (para. 86).

What does this mean in practice? To use an analogy, imagine I turn up late to an important meeting. When my boss asks me why I'm late, I say that it was *because of* the bus. The bus was late, *effectively causing me* to show up late at the meeting. One reading of the approach set out above is that even *if* additional circumstances strongly influence the inability to decide – for example, relational dynamics, such as mistreatment and coercion – then these would *not* be sufficient reasons for a finding of incapacity under the MCA. This suggests that practitioners should not consider the *actual circumstances* of a person's situation, but focus mainly on whether mental impairment – what's in a person's head – affects her decision-making ability. The conditions of mental capacity should therefore be divorced from the individual's real-life context.

To use the example of Margo, this approach would focus narrowly on whether her Alzheimer's condition impacts on her ability to make a decision about remaining at home and continuing to live with her son. How does her mental impairment affect her deliberation: is she able to retain and understand the relevant information about the risks/benefits of having contact with her son? Can she use and weigh it and communicate a decision? Concerns about her son's coercive and potentially abusive conduct could only play a very limited a role in the capacity assessment. Any finding of incapacity has to be *because* her Alzheimer's prevents her from passing the functional test. Even if she freely divulges being fearful of her son (an admission of his undue influence) and admits to how this fear aggravates her confusion (how this undue influence impacts on her impairment), these factors would have no bearing on the capacity assessment, particularly if during the test there is little or no evidence that her impairment is directly impacting on her cognitive processes (such as confusion about the information or forgetfulness during the period of assessment). Applying a very narrow version of the causative nexus, Margo has capacity, thereby dramatically altering the nature of the steps it might be possible to take to secure her interests.

From a strict legal perspective, one might argue that this approach provides an important clarification as to which cases fall within or outside the scope of the MCA. It also seemingly provides much more latitude for individuals to make 'unwise choices' – a freedom that should be accorded to those with impairments.

The approach, however, does have rather puzzling implications. It appears to advocate that practitioners take individuals with impairments as isolated minds, removed from relationships and bodily interactions within their physical and social world. To use the tardiness example, this would be like my boss viewing my *hypothetical* decisions and actions as effectively causing my lateness (*if* I had left early enough, I would have been on time), to the exclusion of *actual circumstances* (like the bus not turning up on time, or being stuck in heavy traffic due to an accident, or my partner failing to fix my bicycle as promised, or the childminder cancelling last minute and the need to scramble for other arrangements). Despite the mundane nature of this example, even here divorcing our decisions and actions from actual circumstances can have serious consequences. If my boss doesn't take into consideration any of these factors, she might actually decide that my tardiness is grounds for dismissal. But most of us are unlikely to think such an approach to be fair or appropriate or even commonsensical – the context matters. Likewise, and more pertinently, the context matters when we have to make decisions that affect our lives in profound ways, like who to marry, or where to live, or whether or not to have treatment for a life-threatening condition.

Importantly, we suggest that it is possible to take a different – broader – approach, while still remaining within the four walls of the MCA. We highlight here *Re BKR* [2015] SGCA 26, a case decided by the Singapore Court of Appeal. Singapore's Mental Capacity Act 2008 (SMCA) is (materially for these purposes) an exact replica of that within England and Wales. In *Re BKR*, and for purposes of interpreting the relevant provisions of the SMCA, the Singapore Court of Appeal analysed the *York* decision in detail and held that evaluations of capacity would have little traction if the specifics of a person's context and situation were removed from consideration. '[M]ental impairment may in some instances affect decision-making ability only in conjunction with P's actual circumstances', leading to the conclusion that 'the court *must* take into account P's circumstances in assessing his mental capacity' (para. 120).[8]

The Singapore Court of Appeal outlined three conditions where the dynamics of a relationship – such as the actual or possible presence of undue influence – would be pertinent to assessments of mental capacity:

1. Whether the individual can retain, understand, or use the information that relates to whether there might be undue influence being applied, e.g., whether she can grasp that another person may have interests contrary to hers, and if not, whether this inability is caused by mental impairment.

2. Whether the individual is vulnerable to undue influence due to mental impairment, where her will is overborne in such a manner that she is unable to use and weigh the relevant information.

3. Whether an individual cannot realistically hope to obtain assistance in making decisions, where a finding of incapacity is because of the interplay between mental impairment and the lack of support (paras. 125–126).

Though this judgment comes from a different legal jurisdiction, we suggest that sets out an approach that it is entirely legitimate

---

8   The Singapore Court of Appeal considered that this was, in fact, what the Court of Appeal had held in the York case, and that the Court of Protection had also held the same in two earlier cases: *Re A (Capacity: Refusal of Contraception)* [2010] EWHC 1549 (Fam) and *The London Borough of Redbridge v G and Others* [2014] EWHC 485 (COP).

for practitioners in England and Wales to adopt given that: (1) it represents by far the most complete analysis of the interrelationship between impairment and the actions of others; and (2) it expressly seeks to do this within the framework of an Act materially identical to the MCA.

The *Re BKR* decision highlights a crucial issue. Behind both the MCA and the CRPD is a call to provide support and assistance to individuals so that they can make decisions which affect their lives and can be equal participants in social and political activities. However, directly contradicting this view of supportive decision-making is the picture that can be painted on the basis of what it means to be a decision-maker: an isolated being whose decisions are reached purely in one's head, regardless of the surrounding context. Stated more bluntly, the picture of a capacitous decision-maker is fundamentally rigged against persons with impairments, providing little space, in reality, for the relational supports and mechanisms that are needed to help realise their decision-making abilities.

Thus, we suggest the *Re BKR* judgment is right to recommend a more holistic view of persons with impairment. Rather than isolated minds, denuded of all complex factors which shape their personal identity, these embodied, unique individuals are *embedded within relationships and actual circumstances*. As such, the *interplay* between the individual and complexities within her context, including the quality and nature of her relationships (whether they apply coercion and undue influence, whether they can realistically provide assistance and support for the individual), should be considered in evaluations of decision-making capacity.

To return to the example of Margo, this more holistic approach would view the relational dynamic between her and her son as highly relevant to the question of Margo's mental capacity. Questions would be asked as to whether her son's undue influence *worsens* her ability to use and weigh information, whether she can understand that her son's actions and interests might differ from her own, and whether her son can provide any assistance to her in making decisions about her living arrangements. The interaction between Margo's Alzheimer's and her actual circumstances – her relationship with her son and isolation from others, the squalid conditions of her home – would be contributing factors that practitioners would consider in their assessment.

We suggest that this approach legitimately allows us to avoid an overly narrow interpretation of the causative nexus. Further, the judgment's recognition that one's circumstances can impact on decision-making helps enrich the framework of capacity by accommodating how individuals with impairments are embedded within relationships that can make a material difference to their agency and decision-making abilities. As we will explore in this book, accommodating such complexity is crucial because it means we ignore neither the fact that such a support network might be absent and practitioners may be obliged to help foster that network, nor how a person's capacity can be enhanced through relationship. Remaining wedded to a picture of decision-making that is based entirely on the isolated mind risks judging those who require support as *permanently* falling short of the threshold of capacity – a possibility that ultimately contravenes the empowering ethos behind the MCA and CRPD.

We should emphasise that our book is designed for those who are operating within the MCA. It will therefore always be necessary for any capacity assessment to identify how the relevant impairment or disturbance in the functioning of the person's mind or brain is said to cause the inability to make the decision in question. The reasoning adopted by the Singapore Court of Appeal in *Re BKR* – we suggest – can equally be adopted by those assessing capacity in England and Wales. However, and as we discuss further below (in particular in Chapter 6), this has two very important consequences:

- Adopting this reasoning may well make it easier to find that a person with a cognitive impairment enmeshed in a complex relationship lacks capacity to make material decisions.

- Such a determination can only be legitimate where it is recognised that a crucial part of any best interests decision or action is taken with a view to securing either the gaining or return of the individual's decision-making capacity by ensuring that she is surrounded by the support that she requires.

Although our book is aimed at those who are operating within the four walls of the MCA, we emphasise that many claims about the MCA are themselves not enshrined in law but represent pervasive assumptions that can and should be challenged. We argue that the reflections we set out in the chapters that follow are both consistent with the legislation and the intent behind it. Rather than reduce questions of capacity to cognitive, mental processes, this book urges practitioners to consider how mental capacity can also be *relational* – meaning that our ability to make decisions requires a number of skills and abilities that are fostered within supportive contexts and relationships. Navigating the complex, difficult terrain around capacity and best interests demands a more holistic view of the individual, especially if an ethic of enablement and empowerment is to run through our professional practices of care, assessment and advocacy.

Outline of the book

First, a note on language: throughout this book we use the female pronoun in the recognition that even today our language still veers towards the use of the male pronoun. Ideally, we would have liked to avoid the use of either, fully conscious of the fluidity of these gender categories, but the impulse towards grammatical correctness leads us to use 'she' rather than 'they' when speaking of a singular individual.

Moreover, we use the term 'impairment' rather than 'disability' throughout the book: these two concepts are controversial on many levels. From a social model of disability view, the use of 'impairment' is preferable, mainly to denote certain factual biological features of the body and to distinguish from 'disability', which is thought to be caused by environmental/social/political structures. But in other models of disability, such as the International

Classification of Disability (see Chapter 6), the term impairment refers to problems of body functioning which implies deviation or loss – a view that differs substantially from the neutrality of 'impairment' within the social model of disability. We are mindful of these differences and though we have our reservations about the social model, we nonetheless use the terms 'impairment' and 'disability' in accordance with this approach.

The purpose of our book is to provide practical, reflective guidance to practitioners on some crucial complexities within the practice of capacity and best interests assessment. Each chapter covers one area of complexity that we think will be important in light of a more relational approach to capacity. We use examples, case studies and questions to foster critical reflection of one's own professional practices. Most of the case studies relate to decisions made by the Court of Protection, and we have deliberately chosen these to show how the relevant issue has been thought about when it has reached the court. We do not necessarily say that each decision is one that we agree with, and we point out some which we consider to be questionable.

Chapter 2 examines what autonomy means. Most practitioners understand decision-making capacity as the gatekeeper of auto-nomy and have ideas about what it means to respect personal autonomy, but we encourage some critical reflection on certain assumptions around the concept, such as the idea of individual self-sufficiency and independence. Instead, we introduce two key nuances to autonomy: the importance of *relational autonomy* – how relationships and the social context can facilitate autonomy skills – and *absorbed coping*: how perception, emotion and the body interact and cope with one's environment. Incorporating these two aspects into our concept of autonomy will help practitioners become more attuned to the conditions and experiences of impairment and disablement.

Chapter 3 explores two key questions: why do relationships matter to the decision-making capacity of individuals and what kinds of skills and competencies do those *around* the person with impairment need to have in order to be supporting, enabling and empowering influences? We examine in more detail the specific practices and narratives of those relationships which can enhance and promote the capacity of individuals with impairments. The very nature of the functional test of capacity tends to focus more on the competencies of the individual whose capacity is in question. However, when we consider how relationships affect capacity, our focus will need to shift towards the various abilities of those *around* the individual with impairment.

Chapter 4 poses the questions. How can practitioners (1) distinguish between narratives that are enabling or disabling and (2) consciously engage in narrative practices that encourage and empower a person's decision-making abilities? Certain narratives can have an impact on decision-making capacity: for instance, diminishing, denigrating narratives affect the range of choices that one envisages; they impact on the process in which individuals make decisions. The unique perceptual and cognitive challenges among those with impairment amplify the significance of surrounding narratives. We explore the importance of guarding against harmful stigmatising views about impairment where individuals are reduced to their diagnosis, and also discuss the kinds of narratives that encourage a person's authentic self-expression and autonomy.

Chapter 5 discusses the ethical role of assessors and urges reflection on the ethical dimensions to capacity and best interests assessment. There are two dangers that arise in assessment, such as the inconsistent justification for interventions into the lives of individuals against their wishes and the exacerbation of power inequalities. To alleviate these dangers, we critically examine: (1) the *presuppositions* of assessment; (2) the *interactions* of assessment; (3) the *reparative potential* of assessment.

Chapter 6 questions the stark boundary between capacity and best interests. We discuss how both form part of a spectrum: a finding of incapacity does not automatically mean that the individual's views are not important, nor does a finding of capacity mean that the obligations to support and assist individuals somehow no longer apply.

Finally, Chapter 7 briefly summarises the implications of our analysis for practitioners. We encourage practitioners to reflect on a holistic view of the person as situated within actual circumstances and relationships, so that any proposed interventions are sensitive to how the individual interacts with her environment and relational context.

Chapter 2

What is Autonomy?

The ideal of autonomy

Autonomy remains a cornerstone value in our society. Autonomy embodies the right to make our own decisions and determine the direction of our life. It represents the ability to make choices, ranging from mundane everyday ones, like what we choose to eat or wear, to profound far-reaching decisions, like what religion or creed to follow or who to marry.

Autonomy is a core ideal in clinical and social care practice. In the clinical context, patient autonomy means treatments can only be provided if an individual freely consents to it. For example, because of the importance of personal autonomy, clinicians have to honour a Jehovah's Witness patient's right to refuse life-saving blood transfusion based on her personal convictions. Likewise in a social care context, professionals working with elderly individuals often speak of protecting the autonomy of those who wish to remain at home rather than go into care.

Despite how much can be at stake, those working in social and clinical care and legal practice often do not stop to ask themselves precisely what 'autonomy' means. Alternatively, if they do, they can give it what we believe is an unduly narrow definition, asking, in essence, whether a person has an abstract ability to make choices which are to be respected, without probing how and why those choices may be being made. We suggest that we need to take a step back and ask how we can understand the meaning of the term so that it is *inclusive and non-discriminatory* against those with impairments. This chapter suggests that this inclusivity can be achieved by practitioners considering more carefully the importance of support provided by relationships and communities, as all of these are crucial mechanisms which help those with impairments to realise genuine autonomy over their lives.

In this chapter, we want to examine and challenge the common assumptions that frequently lie behind practitioners' understanding of autonomy. Ultimately, we suggest, the concept of autonomy is much more complex than we often presume, and both our capacity adjudications and best interests determinations ought to accommodate these nuances if we are to take into account the necessary supports for individuals with impairments. With our examination, practitioners will be equipped with important critical and reflective tools to refine how autonomy is understood and used in this context.

Three assumptions about autonomy

When practitioners talk of 'respecting a person's autonomy', a trio of assumptions typically underlie their conception of 'autonomy':

- *Individualism:* autonomy focuses on the *individual* and her choices.

- *Cognitive:* it requires some kind of internal, cognitive ability and intellectual skills.

- *Non-interference:* respecting the autonomy of an individual means we don't interfere in her choices, no matter how harmful they might be.

The first assumption is embedded in the idea of autonomy as 'personal self-governance', meaning that individuals are free to pursue their own desires and plans, to hold certain views, make their own choices, and act according to their own beliefs and values. Autonomy so understood focuses on the individual and the choices she makes; it presents the self as a bounded entity that makes self-sufficient choices which are removed from any broader social or cultural context. Or, as it was once said to one of us, this model of autonomy suggests we are all RoboCop, isolated in impervious shells.

The second assumption suggests that to make autonomous decisions demands certain cognitive skills of deliberation and reflection. I must, first, be able reflect on my choices so as to be able to say that they are *authentically mine* – in other words that they reflect who I am, my beliefs and values. For example, I might want to watch a film rather than study for an exam. I might think about my desires here and reflect on the fact that I strongly value doing well in my education. But if I watch the film knowing I can't actually endorse or identify with my decision, there is a question of whether I am actually acting autonomously, given that this choice isn't consistent with my deeper values. It might not reflect my true self or my understanding of who I am. On this approach, autonomy also includes the cognitive ability to make *rationally consistent* choices – where I think about the options, compare the benefits, risks and consequences, and make a choice which accords with my assessment of my relative value. Again, to use the example of watching a film or studying for an exam, I might say to you that I value my education and know that I need to study if I am to live consistently with this value. But if I still choose to watch the film, fully aware of the consequences and knowing that it contradicts my deeper values, it looks as if something might have gone wrong with my reasoning. I say that I want to do well in my education, I knows that I have to study to achieve this, yet I do something entirely different. The reasoning is inconsistent – and we may then say that the person's decision is not autonomous.

The emphasis on the individual and her abilities to make an authentic and consistent choice lead to the third assumption of *non-interference*: autonomy means we don't interfere with a person's decisions, so long as it doesn't interfere with the freedom of others. When we speak of the right of autonomy, it is often used to demarcate a boundary between individuals, as a virtual shield or 'keep out' sign to protect individuals from outside intrusions. You might disapprove of my choices but my autonomy means you cannot force me to study, remove me from a harmful relationship, impose healthy food on me, and so on. You might think those are the 'right' and 'good' things to do, but respect for my autonomy means you cannot interfere with my choices, beliefs and values. Autonomy and the qualities it embodies are separate from questions about what the good life might be, what choices are valuable or worthwhile, and so on. It reserves judgement towards these types of questions.

Despite how common these assumptions are, it is important that practitioners are cautious in assuming that this is all that needs to be said about autonomy. This is especially true when we consider the complex supportive mechanisms that may be required for those with specific impairments to realise their potential for autonomy. The law already recognises that individuals with impairments require support to exercise and realise their autonomy. A core principle of the Mental Capacity Act 2005 (MCA, s1(3)) is the importance of support in helping individuals make their own decisions, while the CRPD emphasises the importance of societal, economic and structural supports so that those with impairments can exercise their legal capacity (i.e., their rights to be respected as individual actors) on an equal basis with others. However, emphasis on the provision of supports and accommodations for individuals to exercise a true form of autonomy sits uneasily with some of the common assumptions outlined above.

We will explore in subsequent chapters where we think the provision of supports and accommodations can take us. However, as a starting point, we suggest that practitioners ought to be more sceptical about these three assumptions when the issue of autonomy crops up. Dangers can emerge if these are accepted without reflection: on the one hand, we can adopt too demanding a view which excludes those who struggle with making decisions by themselves, through some rational, cognitive process. For example, a woman with dementia might need others to prompt her with the pros and cons as to where she should live, and in fact, she may rely heavily on others to guide her through the deliberative process. If we assume she has to think through these issues *herself*, in *her own head*, and entirely in isolation, to be autonomous, we might unjustifiably conclude she lacks capacity to make a decision. On the other hand, it could be too undemanding, in that it means we never intervene in a person's choice so long as she can appear able to rationally deliberate in a consistent manner, even if it is a choice that means the person stays in a deeply neglectful care environment or a disabling relationship. For example, a young man with a learning impairment might appear to deliberate in a consistent manner when he decides he wishes to remain in his father's abusive care.

Moreover, the entirely laudable trend towards requiring greater weight to be placed on the expressed wishes and feelings of those who are found to lack capacity brings with it the risk that we simply defer to those wishes and feelings (Ruck Keene and Auckland 2015; Law Commission 2017). In some cases, however, we may need to take steps (on behalf of others) which may appear on the face of it to clash with those wishes and feelings but in reality are taken to support and enable them to maximise their autonomy.

We therefore risk both saying that those with certain learning and cognitive impairments lack autonomy, and at the same time standing back and allowing objectively harmful choices that may impair and compromise a person's future autonomy. An unduly narrow concept of autonomy risks at the same time both *excluding* individuals with impairments from respect for their decisions and potentially *sanctioning* their mistreatment and abuse. Importantly, and as we will return to, it is increasingly clear that this is so whether we look at matters through the prism of capacity assessment or through the prism of best interests determinations.

A lot therefore rides on getting the concept of autonomy right if considerations of capacity and best interests are to be fair but appropriately nuanced, taking the person and her context into proper consideration. We suggest that practitioners can do this by thinking about autonomy in the following way:

- The choice practitioners face isn't always going to be between paternalistic interference or non-interference, but around how we might *promote and respect* autonomy in individuals.

- Non-rational aspects through which individuals with impairments cope and interact with their environment have a role to play in manifesting their autonomy (i.e., perception, emotion, the body).

- Relationships and the social context matter in terms of whether individuals feel empowered and enabled to make decisions to determine their own lives.

Respecting versus promoting autonomy

It is very common to think that *respecting* a person's autonomy demands *not interfering* with those choices. When someone says, 'respect my right to autonomy', it implies a line can be drawn between my own choices and whether you can tell me what I can or cannot do. Autonomy so understood underlies influential interpretations of Article 12 of the CRPD, in particular, the clause which states that measures relating to the 'exercise of legal capacity' must 'respect the rights, will and preferences of the person'. (For more on the CRPD, see Chapters 1 and 6.) Gerard Quinn argues that Article 12 'opens up zones of personal freedom' and 'facilitates uncoerced interactions' so that individuals with impairments can exercise their right of autonomy and self-determination free of the paternalistic interference of others (Quinn 2010). Particularly if a person doesn't consent to the interference of others, she has a right to make her own mistakes (what is frequently referred to as 'the dignity of risk'), and her choices – even personally harmful ones – ought to be respected.

The logic underlying this view is this: people who don't have disabilities have their right to autonomy respected – they are allowed to make their own mistakes, choose their own relationships, regardless of how unwise or detrimental they might be. They are free to remain in or leave a physically or emotionally abusive relationship, or live in a neglectful environment. The essence of autonomy is equivalent to the right to make choices that are free from the intrusion of others. If we are to treat those with impairments *equally and on par* with those without disabilities, respect for their autonomy should denote the same non-interference. Persons with impairments have been all too often forced to accept paternalistic care against their will, and proper respect for their autonomy would thus mark an important step towards recognising the fundamental equality of *all* individuals.

Advocates of CRPD Article 12 have a powerful point: practitioners need to be aware that persons with impairments deserve the 'dignity of risk', particularly as the impulse to protect them can often cloud judgements about appropriate and inappropriate interventions. Likewise, the historical denial of autonomy to those with mental disorders, learning impairments, psychosocial challenges, often in the name of their best interests, has led to shameful abuses and appalling forms of paternalistic mistreatment at the behest of the state and well-intentioned clinicians. However, while we should be mindful about this history, it also has to be balanced with an ethical, principled stance towards questions of interference and non-interference. Simply arguing that able-bodied individuals are free to make their own personal choices without the interference of others is not a principled stance towards these issues as they apply to those with impairments.

In the first instance, it is not true. Rape, for example, can be prosecuted whether or not the victim supports prosecution, if such is in the public interest (Crown Prosecution Service 2012). The boundary between individual choice and outside intervention can be elastic and permeable even for those who are considered to lack any form of disability. In fact, advocates against domestic violence and child abuse often suggest the need for *more* rather than less intervention in what is traditionally deemed the private sphere, combined with better support and meaningful options, if victims are to be better protected. If non-interference is the last word when we respect a person's autonomy, it could in effect *perpetuate* the abuse or inequality of groups which require substantive supports to be treated equally in any meaningful sense. Indeed, the CRPD itself recognises this in Article 16, which requires that states take 'all appropriate legislative, administrative, social, educational and other measures to protect persons with impairments, both within and outside the home, from all forms of exploitation, violence and abuse, including their gender-based aspects'.

Practitioners therefore need to consider how an over-emphasis on non-interference can neglect the provision of positive supports that allow individuals to develop and realise their autonomy skills. When we talk about *promoting* autonomy it suggests something slightly different to that of *respecting* autonomy. Promoting something implies *acting for, elevating, encouraging*. Going back to the example of domestic abuse, a policy based on non-interference effectively sanctions and approves of these harmful relationships – it says that these are private matters between individuals and the state, law and the community should let private citizens get on with their own business. The absence of external mechanisms of support further signals to victims that they have no other options. Without safe houses, an economic safety net, stronger legal rights and mechanisms for prosecution to protect victims, and the support of people in their community, their surrounding environment ends up reinforcing narratives of powerlessness and helplessness within the abusive setting. Victims of domestic abuse often don't leave an abusive context due to the absence of positive supports which *enable* and *promote* their autonomy, particularly in the future.

Protection and proactive support, even when unwanted, or when a person 'consents to' or is 'happy' remaining in a neglectful, abusive situation, isn't always contrary to respecting the autonomy of individuals. For instance, there may be cases where to *respect* the person's autonomy means we need to remove her from a deeply disabling care environment even in the face of her expressed wishes, if we can properly do so within the legal framework as it stands (see Case study 1). But there will always be finely balanced cases; we should certainly make clear that we are not saying that interventions in the name of promoting future autonomy are *always* right (Case study 2). There will be numerous conditions that need to be considered, as discussed in this chapter and throughout the remainder of the book. But it is important that practitioners are mindful of how they are thinking about autonomy, particularly in guarding against the assumption that considerations of autonomy mean that practitioners are prevented from *promoting* it through appropriate interventions and positive support.

Case study 1

A young man with autism spectrum disorder, WMA, lived an isolated and insular life with his mother, MA, who had sight and mobility problems. Social workers were concerned about the impact of his isolation on his long-term development, and on what they saw as an unhealthy degree of interdependence. They were also concerned at his mother's apparent inability to accept care required to ensure that her son was not neglected. All concerned, including his mother, considered that he lacked capacity to decide whether to continue living with her. The social workers involved in his case came to the reluctant conclusion that it was in his best interests for him to be moved into supported living accommodation, despite the difficulty of the initial move, not least because in the long term this would help the son and his mother to develop a more healthy relationship. WMA, although lacking capacity, was capable of expressing strong and clear views: he wanted to live 'permanently' with his mother, did not want the level of support said to be necessary by the council, and did not like mixing with other people. The court identified that it had before it an 'agonising choice', as to extent to which it should interfere with the man's life with his mother, and move him to a place which, at least at that time, he 'emphatically' did not wish to go.

The lead social worker in WMA's case made the following testimony:

> It is my professional view that WMA is a 23-year-old man with the potential to lead a more fulfilling life. I am also of the view that MA is not deliberately abusive to him but rather has needs of her own that have not been assessed but which impact on her ability to care for WMA effectively and to manage

her own living environment. I think she is not aware that her behaviour towards him is abusive. She has few expectations of him and there is evidence of the frustration she experiences from undertaking his care – shouting at him, preventing him from leaving the property. MA has stated on many occasions she does not want local authority involvement with the family, blaming them for the lack of diagnosis of WMA as a child. She has been found to be neglectful through safeguarding adults' procedures. I am concerned that WMA has been treated in an inhumane and degrading manner by MA and that his true potential has been unrecognised and stifled. In order for him to live safely and to have a more fulfilling life, I think he should move on to supported accommodation while continuing to have contact with his mother.

Ultimately, after a careful examination of the evidence, the court concluded that it was in WMA's best interests to move so as to seek to secure for him a better quality of life (including private life), but only on the basis that the local authority took steps to ensure that he continued to see his mother regularly.

(Taken from the decision of HHJ Cardinal in A Local Authority v WMA & MA [2013] EWCOP 50.)

Case study 2

A married couple both had psychiatric conditions. They had a long-standing and committed relationship and they loved one another dearly. The couple had a long history of travel round the country, and on some occasions presented as homeless. Their living circumstances (together and, on occasion, separately) caused increasing concern to the local authority. On a number of occasions the husband had left the woman in various places around England and she had had to be rescued. The woman was placed in a care home, into which the husband moved for a while before the placement broke down and he returned to his own flat. The wife spent increasing amounts of time at the flat, which was described as 'exceptionally insanitary', and declined a request from the local authority to stay six nights a week at the care home.

The court concluded that, although she was 'likeable, highly intelligent, sophisticated and articulate, well read and knowledgeable,' with a high level of intellectual understanding, she was 'simply unable' to use and weigh the risks of the harm that she would suffer if she resumed living with her husband or had uncontrolled contact with him. The judge therefore directed that she be accommodated on an interim basis at the care home, where the judge recognised that she was to be deprived of her liberty, and that the woman would only have accompanied visits to see her husband. The judge made clear that she would have reached the same conclusion even if she had found the wife to have capacity to decide whether to live with her husband.

(Taken from the decision of Parker J in Re PB [2014] EWCOP 14.)

Note: we have deliberately chosen both of these cases because they represent very difficult decisions brought to the court to decide. Our view is that the decision in the first was the right side of the line but that the latter was the wrong side of the line; we invite readers to read the full decisions in both cases and decide whether – and why – they agree or disagree with us.

Absorbed coping and impairment

Much of how we talk about autonomy and decision-making stresses the cognitive, rational and intellectual skills at the moment of making an important decision. The functional test contained in the MCA isn't immune to these assumptions either – 'use and weigh' often denotes the ability to compare the different choices and their consequences, and make a logically consistent choice based on this process of rational comparison.

But this view of autonomous decision-making paints an oddly disembodied picture of a person, as if the mind somehow functions independently of other important features of human beings, such as emotion (how we feel), perception (how we are attuned to certain things in our environment), and embodiment (how our bodily needs interact with our mind). We risk having an unrealistic view of how we engage with the world if these aspects of decision-making and autonomy are neglected. In other words, if our ideal of autonomy comprises disembodied, able-bodied (and typically male) traits, we will miss the ways in which those with different ways of interacting with their environment actually display skilful ways of coping which contribute to their autonomy. Reasoning and reflective thinking remain important skills for the exercise of autonomy, but we cannot minimise the importance of non-rational aspects of agency. If we can reflect this in our practice, we will have a concept of autonomy that attends to and includes the experiences of those with impairment.

When we think of autonomy, there is a tendency to privilege the rational, the thinking process, the moments of making important, deliberative choices. But this obscures the grounding role of our perceptual skills, of our embodied ways of having contact and engaging with the world. At a basic level, our bodies seek connection with the world, with others, and become socially inscribed with meaning as a result. A baby imitates her mother's smile even before she can make any observations about her own face, or of how it might resemble her mother's; a child learns how to perceive and pay attention to features of her environment based on what others around her attend to and focus on. Our bodies, from the very beginning, are frequently geared towards interaction with our environment and with others. Our ways of communicating, through touch, movement, speech and facial expression attest to the fact that we are not solitary thinking machines, but embodied, engaged, social beings who often perceive features of our environment and react to them in a manner that feels intuitively right to us.

A powerful way of looking at the autonomy of individuals with impairments is through the model of *absorbed coping*: the perceptual skills of everyday bodily engagement with one's environment (Dreyfus 2014). 'Coping' implies the ability to adapt to and manage the demands of our environment in our everyday interaction with the world, while the description 'absorbed' pushes against the idea that individuals retreat into themselves to cope skilfully, effectively disengaging themselves from their environment. The concept of absorbed coping refers to a deeper meaning beyond our normal, everyday understanding. For example, think of how you might respond to someone who asks you how you are managing after a family death – you might say, 'I'm coping alright', which might mean all sorts of things, such as 'I'm still going to work and taking care of the kids', or 'I'm managing to keep my emotions together'. Absorbed coping goes further than these colloquial meanings: it is how we manage to be *comfortable with our environment through perception and bodily interaction with the world, even before we might think and reflect on it*. It's how our body structures and navigates the constraints of our environment, and we act and adjust accordingly, perhaps even without thinking.

Consider, for example, a person who is skilled at playing a musical instrument: a piano player, after years of practice, knows intuitively where to place her fingers to play a scale. If she has to think about it, this in fact represents *a lack or weakness* of skill. A beginner has to think about where the notes are, how to position her hand, how hard to press the keys. But someone who is skilled intuitively knows which keys to press, how to react to playing different types of piano, for example an electric keyboard as opposed to a real piano, where she will automatically adjust the pressure of her fingers to the weight of the keys, reacting immediately when she touches them. The fact that she doesn't think about it represents the extent of her skill.

This type of skilful absorbed coping applies in important ways to individuals with impairments. Faced with incomprehensible or unreasonable behaviours, practitioners may interpret the action of a person with disability as an instance of *poor* coping which requires management or control. But in fact, these behaviours can be examples of effective, purposive coping strategies in dealing with the interaction between one's bodily impairment and the surrounding environment. For example, Naoki Higashida describes beautifully how his autism affects his perception of his surrounding environment and how intuitive bodily action helps him cope. He talks about the importance of jumping to deal with affective distress and the experience of lacking control over his body, stating '[i]t's as if my whole body, except for my soul, feels as if it belongs to somebody else and I have zero control over it' (Naoki 2007, p.68). By contrast:

> When I'm jumping, it's as if my feelings are going upwards to the sky. Really, my urge to be swallowed up by the sky is enough to make my heart quiver. When I'm jumping, I can feel my body parts really well, too – my bounding legs and my clapping hands – and that makes me feel so, so good. So that's one reason I jump, and recently I've noticed another reason. People with autism react to feelings of happiness and sadness. So when something happens that affects me emotionally, my body seizes up as if struck by lightening. 'Seizing up' doesn't mean that my muscles literally get stiff and immobile – rather, it means that I'm not free to move the way I want. So by jumping up and down, it's as if I'm shaking loose the ropes that are tying up my body. (Naoki 2007, pp.76–77)

Those around Naoki might initially find his suddenly jumping a bewildering sight – why is he doing this? How can we make sense of it? It seems like an irrational, random thing to do. But through the lens of absorbed coping, we might begin with the question, how is Naoki's behaviour a *purposive bodily response* to how he perceives his environment, in light of his unique experience of impairment? How could his jumping be an *appropriate and skilful* response from his perspective?

As we will see later, we may end up giving answers to these questions either in the context of asking whether the person has or lacks the capacity to make a specific decision, or in the context of determining what steps may need to be taken in her best interests. But unless we have asked the questions, we will be going wrong from the outset.

Wandering behaviour is another useful example of absorbed coping. On one hand, when someone with autism or an elderly resident with dementia wanders off, it is often assumed to be an automatic impulse that lacks explanation or reason. Or we might focus on possible harms (she could get hurt, she might get lost, she might disturb others) and focus on managing the behaviour. More often than not, wandering isn't associated with autonomous behaviour. But when we begin with this notion of absorbed coping, it can alert us to important ways in which this *is* purposive behaviour, where individuals are attempting to make sense of and interact with unfamiliar features of their environment in light of their bodily impairment. Naoki describes how his wandering behaviour expresses his interest in things within his perceptual field, but also a search for somewhere he can feel at ease in his body:

> I dash off as soon as I spot anything interesting. … We don't really know where we ought to be. … Simply put, people with autism never, ever feel at ease, wherever we are. Because of this, we wander off – or run away – in search of some location where we *do* feel at ease. While we're on this search, it doesn't occur to us to consider how or where we're going to end up. We get swallowed up by the illusion that unless we can find a place to belong, we are going to be all alone in the world. Then eventually we get lost, and have to be escorted back to the place we were at, or the person we were with before. But our uneasy, unsettled feeling doesn't go away (Naoki 2007, pp.129–130).

In the case of wandering dementia residents in long-term care, George Agich clarifies how this behaviour may well reflect a bodily response to being in an unfamiliar environment (Agich 1993). Even when our minds might not reflect on our emotional discomfort or register our perceptions that something is strange and amiss, it is as if our bodies know. All of us – whether we have recognisable impairments or not – rely on non-rational aspects of our body to make sense of and find stability in the world around us. When practitioners recognise this, it challenges the assumption that the actions of Naoki running off or a dementia resident wandering around the care home are manifestations of their fundamentally disabled, incapacitous, non-autonomous bodies. They could be rather, skilful attempts to stabilise themselves in an unfamiliar context, in light of their experience of bodily impairment.

In summary, everyday coping is the necessary framework for those thinking and reasoning abilities that tend to be associated with autonomy. To make the body comfortable and responsive to the environment requires practical skill – and there is a tendency to discount how people with impairments are trying to achieve precisely this in their everyday purposive action. Impairment will affect how the body perceives and interacts with one's environment, but behaviours that seem to be unreflective or irrational at first may be instances of skilful coping to make oneself more comfortable in one's environment, based on one's unique perceptions and bodily experience. With absorbed coping as our starting point, autonomy will better *include* rather than *exclude* the bodily experiences of those with impairments. This isn't all there is to the concept, but it's a good starting point.

Relational autonomy

So far we have stressed the importance of incorporating some non-rational aspects of skilful bodily coping as part of our definition of autonomy. We have discussed how this lends itself to a kind of outward orientation – where our bodies interact with the world and others around us. This also helps us rethink what helps us make autonomous decisions. If our bodily coping, even as early as when we are infants, depends on us perceiving, being open, depending on and interacting with those around us, why would this suddenly be irrelevant as soon as we make decisions? The law recognises the importance of support and help in enabling those with impairments to make decisions about their care and treatment. Yet oddly, we tend to operate on the assumption that autonomy requires individuals to be self-sufficient and independent, focusing entirely on what goes on inside a person's head. Put another way, dependency on others is often perceived to be contrary to autonomy.

But we need to remember that individuals aren't isolated islands. Almost all of us live in a web of interdependency. We rely on our partners to show support, love and care, we depend on our friends to be loyal and kind, we need our communities to give us a sense of place and belonging. This suggests that we need to pay attention to the context around the individual. From the perspective of what is called *relational autonomy*, autonomy is not only developed through socialising forces (i.e., education, family, cultural or religious beliefs) it is also exercised *within* relationship – meaning that we will engage with these socialising forces when forming our values, preferences and choices with others.

We as individuals never make decisions from 'a view from nowhere'. Various social and relational influences make us who we are. For the question of autonomy, what is important is how we become the way we are, how this may or may not cultivate a sense of self which reflects skills that enable us to determine our life in an authentic manner. Part of this will involve a passive process: we don't choose what familial environment we grow up in or the society that surrounds us – we inherit our social, cultural institutions and educative influences. Depending on the level of dependency for their care, those with impairments are particularly vulnerable to environmental conditions. Social messages convey to individuals that they can either trust the ways that their bodies engage and cope with the world, or these are seen as 'problems' or 'obstacles' that require management and strict control. When a person receives positive messages about her value and worth, or the trustworthiness of her bodily reactions and emotion, this helps cultivate a more responsive, confident attitude towards herself and her environment. Think about how a parent encourages her child to choose what to wear, or her teenage son to consult himself and discuss with others about the A-levels he wishes to take, within a framework of safety and acceptance.

These early narratives and relationships are crucial groundwork for developing autonomy skills, and Chapter 4 discusses this in more detail. But these skills are further developed through an active process when we engage and talk with others, when we share our personal thoughts and feelings, moving back and forth from our social, relational context and ourselves. Conversation and dialogue will be important because they invite a less insular manner of learning about ourselves and what is important to us. The fact is that we can be wrong about ourselves, be unaware about inconsistencies in our thinking and motives, or have imperfect knowledge about our situation. Dialogue and conversation with others could help rectify many of these issues, and, indeed, make us further aware of some tensions which exist within ourselves and the expectations of our community and relationships. Open dialogue with others allows us to test our beliefs about ourselves, circumstances, values and choices, and helps encourage a kind of self-understanding and self-knowledge that is needed for autonomy. By contrast, when we are closed off from others and refuse to enter into dialogue and conversation, it could indicate oppressive social and relational circumstances that discourage the authentic, flexible and dynamic exploration of ourselves, which then hamper the development of autonomy skills. It means we fail to engage in the active process of developing the skills needed to be autonomous agents.

In summary, relationships can impact on how we see ourselves. They can affect whether or not we actually have developed skills of reasoning, reflection and trusting our bodily interactions with the world, whether we have the tendency to consult our emotions, values and feelings in making decisions, and whether we have the motivation to follow through on these. An individualistic assumption of autonomy suggests that self-determination demands that we *disengage* and *remove* ourselves from social influences which make us who we are – I need to abstract from the influences that make me who I am, like my cultural or family history, my social background, my relationships, so I act from this authentic, oddly isolated core. By contrast, relational autonomy believes this is an impossible task. Our family history, our relationships, the social context, all help form who we are, and where we end and the influence of others begins is often extremely difficult to separate.

But it is *how* the individual engages with the influences of others that is the point of interest.

From the standpoint of relational autonomy, then, we can be interdependent beings and still make decisions that demand respect as our own. Connection with others is essential for autonomy to flourish. Building these connections and interdependent bonds helps create an environment that accepts and fosters different ways of skilful bodily coping, encouraging the more challenging skills of self-understanding and conversation with others so that individuals can make autonomous decisions. The opposite is also true: our autonomy is vulnerable to the discouragement, neglect and abuse of those around us. This indicates that something deeper is at stake here in getting our operating concept of autonomy right in mental capacity assessment. Understanding autonomy as situated within relationship means that practitioners could have tools to make important distinctions between those relationships that support or obstruct a person's autonomy skills. It provides a crucial conceptual framework through which we can think about and assess the *history* behind certain values and beliefs, and to evaluate whether these values and beliefs are authentic to the person expressing them.

Consider this example:

Rob experienced his first severe schizophrenic episode when he was 17 years old and was subsequently hospitalised. At the time, his mother insisted that he remain within her care following his discharge and likewise resisted any social care assistance, claiming that she knew what was best for her son. Her care has been loving but overbearing. Now in his 50s, Rob struggles to carry out basic tasks, such as change batteries or adjust the thermostat, due to years of hearing narratives of his dependency and helplessness. His elderly mother has now become physically enfeebled and, due to the enmeshed nature of their relationship, he panics about the prospect of his mother dying. When offered a choice to moving to independent, supported living, he decides to remain in his mother's home because he believes he will be helpless without her. (example modified from Kong 2017)

Imagine that you as a practitioner need to determine whether Rob has the capacity to make a decision about his living arrangements, and discussion turns to Rob's autonomy. If autonomy is based purely on the ability to make rationally consistent decisions that accord with one's beliefs and values, then it would appear that Rob's choice reflects his authentic wishes: his preference to remain with his mum is consistent with his belief that he would be helpless without her. It wouldn't matter how he acquired those beliefs – of whether these stem from years of hearing narratives of his helplessness. Practitioners could conclude that Rob has decision-making capacity, particularly if he insists that he has considered the prospect of his mother dying and the consequences of him staying where he is.

But practitioners might well find this conclusion unsettling. Many assessments of capacity revolve around issues of trying to ensure that someone *maintains* or doesn't *lose* her decision-making capacity. Our suggestion is that the concept of relational autonomy helps provide richer tools to understand and assess how Rob acquired his beliefs and values and the ways in which he engages with the potentially problematic relational, social or cultural influences that go into the very formation of his identity, narratives and manner of reasoning. Perhaps with some further dialogue with his social worker, Rob might acknowledge that if he had been left to his own devices without his mother's intervention, he would have likely accepted social care support for independent living much earlier in his life. This dialogue would be important in drawing attention to his own uneasiness with how he acquired beliefs about his helplessness and a possible tension within himself. From this perspective, Rob's autonomy might be compromised or weakened because his relational context has failed to promote the skills that are needed to make self-determining choices.

Whether this means – in the specific context of English law – that it is legitimate to intervene on the basis that Rob lacks decision-making capacity is a different question, to which we will return in Chapter 6. However, we are at this stage concerned simply to make it clear that looking at matters through the prism of relational autonomy allows us to get much closer to the reality of the situation. It is because we think this concept is so important that the whole of the next chapter is devoted to why relationships matter. We conclude this chapter, though, with a table that summarises the key distinctions between the individualistic narrow concept of autonomy and the wider relational view of it that we will develop more in Chapter 3.

Table 1: Distinctions between individualistic and relational autonomy

Individualistic autonomy	Relational autonomy
• Individuals need to be self-sufficient and independent.	• Individuals are embedded within relationships and are interdependent.
• Autonomy requires me to abstract from my family, social and relational context to understand myself and my choices.	• Autonomy requires me to engage with my family, social and relational context, and how this shapes who I am, my beliefs, values and choices.
• Beliefs, values and choices should be explicit and consciously reflected on if they are to be consistent with autonomy.	• Social influences on my beliefs, values and choices can be unconscious and not fully explicit. This can be consistent with autonomy.
• Autonomy skills reflect internal abilities within my head, such as my process of reasoning.	• Autonomy skills encompass socially acquired skills of bodily engagement, perception and emotion, as well as reasoning.
• The surrounding social, cultural and relational context cannot determine whether I can be judged to be autonomous or not.	• The surrounding social, cultural and relational context can sometimes determine whether I can be judged to be autonomous or not.
• Dialogue with others is not necessary to demonstrate autonomy skills.	• Dialogue with others can demonstrate autonomy skills.

Checklist of reflective questions

- Are you *respecting* or *promoting* this person's autonomy?

- How is respecting a person's autonomy *now* going to impede or encourage her *future* autonomy?

- What kinds of supports and accommodations are needed if this person's autonomy is to be promoted now and in the future?

- Are the person's circumstances supporting or disempowering her? What can you do to change those circumstances to support her?

- Do you think that the person would see what you would like to do as supportive of her autonomy? If not, why not, and how could you change your approach?

Chapter 3

Why Relationships Matter

Introduction

We discussed in the previous chapter how relationships help or obstruct personal autonomy. There are two key implications to this.

The first is that relationships matter to the decision-making capacity of individuals: they can be supportive by helping us make crucial choices about our care and treatment, but equally, they can hamper our abilities and be disabling influences. In acknowledging the crucial impact of interpersonal support on autonomy and decision-making capacity, the singular focus on the individual and her cognitive processes in capacity assessment starts to look untenable. Our focus needs to shift towards the abilities and competencies of the circle of support *around* the person with impairment – including family members, practitioners and even capacity assessors. Those who are part of this circle of support will need to possess certain skills if they are to be a respectful, empowering influence that enables decision-making capacity.

The second key implication (which we discuss further in Chapter 6) is that the focus on relationships does not stop merely because a person is – despite our efforts – on the 'other side' of the capacity line drawn by the Mental Capacity Act 2005. If we are taking steps in the name of the person's best interests, we must always remain focused on whether in taking those steps and working with others around that person, we are maximising her autonomy in the sense that was outlined in the previous chapter.

This chapter explores two key questions: first, why do relationships matter to decision-making capacity? Our discussion builds on the previous chapter's exploration of autonomy, where we urged practitioners to adopt a more nuanced view of how autonomy might be expressed in people with impairments. Here, we want to focus more carefully on the ways in which bodily impairment could heighten a person's vulnerability to the enabling or disabling care and treatment of others. Relationships also matter because human rights conventions, particularly the CRPD, rightly emphasise the support and accommodations that must be provided to those with impairments. The second question we pose in this chapter is: what kinds of skills and competencies do those within the circle of support need to develop in order to support, enable and empower individuals with impairments? We will discuss how those within the circle of support need to cultivate certain skills of *interpretation and understanding* in their interactions with an individual with impairments, so that the latter's unique needs, personality and perspective are properly recognised and respected.

Vulnerability and care

Relationships matter because of the varying levels of dependency on and vulnerability to others which persons with impairments experience. The very fact that we are human makes us all vulnerable to some degree – we need nourishment to survive, our bodies can get sick or become weakened. We all experience the giving and receiving of care at different phases in our lives. Importantly, dependency on the care of others doesn't make us helpless or powerless, nor does it mean one lacks autonomy or decision-making capacity. As we discussed in the previous chapter, autonomy can be situated within a web of interdependency – indeed, such a web can help autonomy flourish.

Certain situations and circumstances can nonetheless make us more vulnerable. We might be more susceptible to depression due to marital breakdown or anxiety as a result of a heavy workload, for example. Greater dependency on others for our daily care needs, for the framing of options and our personal abilities, can make us particularly vulnerable to our environment and how others engage with us. Others can worsen or exploit the dependency caused by features of bodily impairment, through practices, policies or actions that exclude, discriminate or abuse. This creates a toxic form of vulnerability, like the systemic discrimination experienced by a person of limited mobility who is denied a wheelchair by government policy, or a woman with dementia who is locked up by the son she depends on for her basic needs. Surrounding narratives and practices can also have a profound effect on an individual's sense of self and abilities, for instance when a person with a learning impairment is consistently told she is stupid or infantilised by her caregivers, to the point she repeats only what they tell her to say. Likewise, a young woman with Rett syndrome will be entirely dependent on others to help her move around, making her particularly vulnerable to how others respond to her immobility. If her carers are overprotective and downplay her abilities to the point that her body atrophies, this would be a toxic form of vulnerability that stems from morally questionable interventions by those around her; by contrast, if her carers help her move around, encourage her to engage in actions that convey her inclusion, value and agency, it shows appropriate responsiveness to her vulnerability in light of her unique bodily needs.

As these examples show, the agency of individuals can be enacted through, or obstructed by others. This places a great deal of responsibility on those within a person's circle of support, for family members and practitioners to provide care, support and encouragement and to respond appropriately to another's vulnerabilities, so that individuals can make and implement decisions that affect their lives. The carers of someone with dementia, for example, might have the responsibility of ensuring the stove is turned off, for reminding her to eat and nourish herself, of alleviating distress as she copes with loss of memory and physical mobility, all to facilitate her choice to remain in the house she loves rather than moving to an impersonal care home. In this situation, whether or not this is a capacitous decision for purposes of the Mental Capacity Act 2005 is neither here nor there – her choice is clear, and those around her are acting to enable her to implement it.

Responsibility falls disproportionately on a care provider in these types of relationships, though this isn't to say that these relationships are fundamentally *unequal* or *non-reciprocal*. We will discuss later how these relationships can be seen as reciprocal (indeed, it is important to think of them as such to challenge certain harmful attitudes and prejudices around those with impairments). But with this greater responsibility comes the need to examine carefully the manner in which others are treated; it demands an awareness of a certain power dynamic and conscious efforts to neutralise it. By virtue of their greater responsibility, those who are part of a person's circle of support need *to themselves acquire and cultivate certain skills and competencies* if individuals with impairments are to be respected and treated as subjects, not objects.

Case study

Ms Manuela Sykes was by nature a fighter, a campaigner, a person of passion. Having been involved in many of the moral, political and ideological battles of the last century, she was now 89 and fighting another battle: dementia. Diagnosed in 2006, she made a living will – prioritising her quality of life over its prolongation – and campaigned for the rights of dementia sufferers. In 2011, she appointed a close friend under a property and affairs Lasting Power of Attorney, stating, 'I would not like my attorney to sell my property. My wish is to remain in my own property for as long as this is feasible.' She had lived in a flat in central London for 60 years.

A culmination of not accepting care, altercations with others, self-neglect, unhygienic and hazardous living condi-tions, weight loss (to 41kg), wandering, and lack of awareness of personal safety, resulted in her compulsory admission to hospital under the Mental Health Act 1983. It was then considered to be in her best interests to be discharged to a nursing home. Ms Sykes was profoundly unhappy in the care home and repeatedly expressed the desire to go home. When the matter came to court, the judge concluded that it was clear that Ms Sykes did not have capacity to make the decision whether or not to go home – her short-term memory was reduced to less than a minute as a consequence of her dementia.

However, District Judge Eldergill noted that that was not the end of the matter, stating:

> It is *her* welfare in the context of her wishes, feelings, beliefs and values that is important. This is the principle of beneficence which asserts an obligation to help others to further their important and legitimate interests. In this important sense, the judge no less than the local authority is her servant, not her master.

Although he took the view that significant problems and some distress might lie ahead in attempting a trial, District Judge Eldergill held that:

> [s]everal last months of freedom in one's own home at the end of one's life is worth having for many people with serious progressive illnesses, even if it comes at a cost of some distress. If a trial is not attempted now the reality is that she will never again have the opportunity to live in her own home. Her home will be sold and she will live out what remains of her life in an institution. She does not want that, it makes her sufficiently unhappy that sometimes she talks about ending things herself, and it involves depriving her of her liberty.

Recognising the importance of Ms Sykes's long-standing values and perspective and the responsibility of others to accommodate these, the judge made an order which had the effect of requiring a trial at home be undertaken.

[adapted from the 39 Essex Chambers report of Westminster City Council v Sykes [2014] EWCOP B9].

Support and human rights

Before we turn to the skills and competencies that the circle of support requires, we should sketch out why they are so important from a different perspective – as a response to the challenge posed by the social model of disability, which is embodied in the human rights framework of the CRPD. This model, at its strongest, claims that there is, in fact, no such thing as disability, simply a societal failure to provide the necessary support to respond to an individual's particular impairments (see Appendix 2). It therefore requires us to focus on *our* responses to the individual with impairments, both at a 'macro' societal level and in our 'micro' interactions with that individual, in both cases to ensure that, so far as possible, we enable that individual to realise her goals on an equal basis with those without impairments. Most of us are already familiar with the idea of 'reasonable adjustment' in the workplace to cater for those with physical disabilities – for instance, widening the doorway to enable a person with a wheelchair easy access to an office.

The CRPD goes further, however, to challenge us to make the same form of adjustments to those with cognitive impairments to support and enable them to make decisions regarding their lives which are recognised on the same basis as others. Advocates of the strongest version of the human rights model of disability deny the validity of mental capacity and hence, by extension, regimes (such as the MCA 2005) which allow decisions to be made for a person on the basis that she does not (at that time) have the mental capacity to do so. We cannot share this view: indeed, denying the differences that arise from impairments – which cannot be removed even with appropriate social support – risks leaving individuals with such impairments in situations that are ethically unjustifiable. We also think that taking this approach ignores the fact that an equally important obligation contained in the CRPD placed on states is to secure protection for persons with disabilities, both within and outside the home, from all forms of exploitation, violence and abuse, including their gender-based aspects.[1]

---

1   In Article 16. See Chapter 1.

We therefore take our approach from the guiding principle in Article 12(3) CRPD that we must provide support to those with impairments to enable them, insofar as is possible, to exercise their legal capacity to be recognised as a subject, not an object. In the context of practice in England and Wales, this encompasses a wide range of steps including, for instance:

- Providing support to enable the person to take her own decision and make her own choice – in other words, following through in the requirement in s.1(3) MCA 2005 that a person is not to be unable to make a decision unless all practicable steps to help her to do so have been taken without success.

- (Where possible) assisting a person to make advance decisions and/or appoint someone to act on her behalf at a point when she cannot make her own decisions.

- Where it is not possible, applying the MCA 2005, to support the person to make her own decision, constructing a best interests decision[2] for her through a process which seeks firstly to identify what decision she wishes to make, and – insofar as possible – to carry into effect her choice.

As we will see further in Chapter 6, there are times when we may need to take steps which do not, on the face of it, seem to respect the person's choice so as to achieve a goal we can justify in the name of the person's *own* rights and interests: and, in particular, to secure and support her long-term agency and autonomy. It is because of the potential risks inherent in this course of action that we need to proceed with such care, and with such attention to the skills that we require. We therefore turn to look in more detail at those skills.

---

2   We take the phrase 'constructing decisions' from the work of Adrian Ward (see, in particular, *Adult Incapacity Legislation*) (Ward 2003).

Hermeneutic competence

So far we have answered the question of *why* relationships are important: first, dependency on others for our care places responsibility on the circle of support to encourage and enable our agency; equally, it can be exploited to become a toxic form of vulnerability that works to exclude, abuse or neglect. Second, a human rights lens demands mechanisms of support to ensure the participation and empowerment of persons with disabilities. Together, these shift what can be a disproportionate focus on the capacities of the *individual* and her impairment, towards the capacities that are needed by her *circle of support*. What capacities, competencies and practices do carers, family members, practitioners and assessors need to have if they are to actively support, include and empower persons with disabilities?

We use the term *hermeneutic competence* to capture the range of skills and practices that those within the circle of support need to cultivate if they are to enable and respect individuals with impairments. 'Hermeneutics' is a technical term that describes the method by which we interpret and confer meaning to words, actions and practices; it explains how we build understanding and dialogue with other points of view that differ from our own. When we read a novel, or interpret how the law applies to a specific case, or engage in conversation with someone, all of these involve hermeneutics. We might read a book by Charles Dickens, but might misunderstand its significance or relevance to our own conditions; we might read a legal statute, but not appreciate how it applies to the particular circumstances of a case. We can interpret and engage in dialogue in ways that enhance our understanding of others, but equally, we can also misinterpret and be shut off from dialogue, preventing us from grasping another's perspective.

The relevance of hermeneutics to capacity and impairment might not be immediately obvious. But consider the common dilemmas that emerge in situations where communication might be a challenge: for example, a practitioner might ask how she ought to respond to the actions of a young man banging his head against the wall in a psychiatric ward. If she assumes this is the patient just acting out, trying to manipulate the staff to get what he wants, or is behaving unreasonably with no purpose, it immediately shuts down any potential understanding of the patient's perspective. It imposes a certain meaning about his actions onto him and forecloses the possibility that she might learn and understand something about him, of where he is coming from. By contrast, if the clinician starts with the position that this is a mode of communication, that the patient is trying to express something about his way of seeing the world, already the channel for communication becomes open because the clinician's interpretive orientation is one of seeking to understand and make sense of the patient's behaviour, from his unique point of view.

The basic idea behind hermeneutics is that we are always engaged in the task of interpreting and understanding others, be it through their actions, behaviours, words or choices. These can be especially bewildering if there is a gulf in physical or perceptual experience. 'Hermeneutical competence' describes what is needed to *bridge this gulf* – it comprises skills that are needed to understand *well* through dialogue in cases where we are prone to *mis*understand, *mis*interpret, or make *in*correct assumptions. These interpretive skills can help frame the way we approach persons with disabilities, so that on the one hand, we don't lose sight of their unique individuality, potential abilities and vulnerabilities, and on the other hand, we take responsibility for our role in communicating in a manner that makes them feel heard, understood and validated. Daily interactions with a person requiring care might range from helping someone decide about what to eat or drink, what to wear and where to go. These interactions seem relatively small, but can have a larger impact, often reflecting and feeding into a general social, cultural and institutional attitude towards those with impairments. The difference between interactions that enable and disable can mean the difference between a nurturing, enabling or stifling, limiting living arrangement, between a society that values and respects or dismisses and disregards persons with impairments. This makes it absolutely vital that this communicating, interpreting and understanding of those with impairments is done *competently*.

Practitioners, family members, care providers and capacity assessors all need to start with the right interpretive orientation based on the three features of hermeneutic competence:

1. *Attunement to impairment:* acknowledging the intrinsic challenges of an individual's impairment without making it define the person.

2. *Recognition of the person:* respect for the individual's separate needs, perspective and views.

3. *Open dialogue and humility:* conversation that reflects critical awareness of one's prejudices and guards against their intrusion on how another person's words and actions are interpreted, while humility overturns the presumption that one knows 'better' than the other.

1 Attunement to impairment

Attunement denotes receptivity, awareness and becoming accustomed to something; it implies acceptance and adaptability. Within the circle of support, such attunement must be cultivated so that everyone recognises the perceptual and bodily challenges caused by a person's impairment. This isn't to say that impairment *defines* the person, nor does it *determine* her capacities or level of inclusion and participation in society. But attunement to impairment requires those within the circle of support to cultivate *acceptance* for a person's unique embodiment and *awareness* of how impairment affects her and her coping behaviours, and to *adapt* their responses to ameliorate these challenges so that they enable the capacities of the person.

Some might say that this kind of attunement lies at the heart of the social model of disability enshrined in the CRPD. As we have seen above, according to the social model of disability nothing is inherently wrong with a person's impairment: individuals who experience psychosocial challenges, learning difficulties or have a particular mental health diagnosis are not 'disabled'. According to the social model, disablement occurs when those with impairments are prevented from participating in social and political life on an equal basis with others because society, institutions and structures fail to accommodate the full diversity of bodily experience. For example, there is nothing 'wrong' with a person who cannot use her legs and relies on a wheelchair to get around. This physical impairment becomes a disability, however, when public transport stations lack lifts, or buildings are designed without ramps. The social model subsequently argues that efforts shouldn't be focused on trying to 'fix' the person but rather, they should work to modify the society to correct exclusionary and discriminatory structures which prevent the full participation of those with impairments in social, cultural and political life (see Appendix 2).

The social model is important to keep in mind for a couple of reasons. First, it rightly challenges the notion that disability always resides within a person's impairment: those within the circle of support need to critically question the notion that, just because one's body or brain works differently, this somehow defines that person's identity, making her 'less than' those who more easily accord with society's expectations. Second, the social model is correct in emphasising the need for substantive changes and accommodations *around* persons with impairment so they are treated as valued, equal citizens. Too often they are viewed as 'lesser', 'slower', 'dumber', 'incapable', 'worthless', simply because society tends to see the diagnosis rather than the person in front of them.

Despite these valuable insights, we think that the social model is nonetheless too sweeping in its view that a person's impairments cannot have residual, disabling effects. Attributing the cause of disablement exclusively to society might actually mean we lose sight of the person and her unique experience of bodily impairment. In this respect, *attunement to impairment* differs slightly from the social model. Being attuned to impairment suggests awareness of how a person's bodily coping might be disabling, even with the most inclusive societal measures to accept and accommodate different levels of ability. The limitations and suffering of bodily impairment could be called 'predicaments' (Shakespeare 2006, p.63). 'Even if environments and transports were accessible and there was no unfair discrimination on the basis of disability,' Tom Shakespeare writes, 'many disabled people would still be disadvantaged' (p.65). Attunement to impairment doesn't reduce individuals to features of their bodily functioning, but demands attending to these 'predicaments', namely how impairment might affect how one perceives, engages and copes with the world, and how this could lead to challenges to being understood and accepted, heightening one's suffering, or feelings of difference, exclusion and isolation.

To understand this, consider how a common world and sense of belonging are created out of shared perceptual experiences of space and time. When we are a foreign visitor to a place in a different time zone, we immediately try to adjust our schedule to the local time zone, even as our bodies might be acclimatised to where we came from across the world. Or think of norms on public transport, like those that dictate which side of the escalator to walk or stand. In London, one walks on the left or stands on the right – and violators of the rule are often picked out as tourists or visitors from outside London. By comparison, in Shanghai, no rule regulates where one should stand or walk on the escalator. How we interact with the space in these contexts can cultivate a sense of shared belonging and common experience (i.e., I might be an out-of-town visitor, but I feel as if I am a Londoner when I walk on the left of the escalator) or can be an experience that is isolating and disorientating (being the recipient of irritation as a tourist standing on the wrong side, or feeling confusion as a Londoner in Shanghai who stands on the right while seeing others standing on both sides of the escalator).

This analogy is useful in capturing how our perceptual interaction with space and time can create or thwart a sense of shared experience and belonging with those around us. The analogy has its limits, however. In the case of the tourist in London, the expectation is that the person will adapt her behaviour to comply with, say the local time zone or which side to stand on public transport, to share in the common world with those around her (not least, to avoid annoying impatient commuters). But in the case of impairment, the expectation that the person adapts her behaviour to accord with societal expectations is fundamentally discriminatory. To this extent, therefore, the social model is self-evidently correct. Equally, however, we need to acknowledge the fact that impairment can profoundly affect how we experience and perceive space and time, making us out of sync with aspects of the consensual common world in a more permanent fashion. It can distort the core perceptual experiences that help us feel connected to others at a basic level, *even with the most inclusive alterations within our environment and society.*

For example, a woman with dementia might grow increasingly distressed as she loses her sensory motor skills and her memory loss worsens, creating genuine suffering for her. Her experience of both space and time has changed as a result of her impairment, often departing from what those around her might experience themselves. She might not be able to leave her house any more and her sense of space has become restricted due to her frailty. Or familiar things in her space might become unfamiliar, affecting how her body interacts with her surrounding environment – she might fall a bit more frequently, become anxious about small, common but unexpected occurrences, or insist on remaining in her bedroom, refusing to leave it. If we assume that her impairment is 'neutral' – all that needs to prevent disablement is to alter structures around her – we will minimise the frustration, pain, discomfort or suffering she feels as a result of her dementia. Crucially, responses that disregard intrinsic 'predicaments' that arise from her condition can worsen rather than ameliorate disablement, even with the best of intentions. Her family might simply take her at face value when she states she is safe at home and, as a result, do nothing to change the layout of furniture to prevent the risk of tripping when she wanders. Moreover, disorientation around her perception of time might not be taken seriously, and hence her carers may be insensitive to how her refusal to bathe might be due to fluctuations in her own daily rhythm that result from her impairment.

In other words, impairments can cause individuals to struggle to adapt and function within certain spaces or common measures of time, and their coping responses – though appropriate given their bodily reality – may be prone to being misunderstood by others. Without any sensitivity and attunement to individuals' impairments, we risk imposing on them the unwarranted expectation that *they* ought to adapt in certain ways which may not be possible, or turning a blind eye to the very real 'predicaments' of impairment, whether it be bodily pain, anxiety, suffering or isolation. And this expectation can worsen an individual's sense of powerlessness, uncertainty, of not belonging in the world and disconnection from others. We fail to establish a common world because we fail to understand how impairment can disrupt perceptual experiences of space and time. It is incumbent on the circle of support around the woman with dementia to become aware and accepting of ways in which her impairment might lead to different experiences of space and time, and its effect on how she manages and expresses herself. The circle of support should seek to understand how the predicaments of her impairment warrant a sensitive, attuned response – adapting the space or manipulating their schedule to alleviate affective distress or lessen confusion. Ultimately, such attunement helps bridge divergent perceptual experiences and establishes a common world with her. This paves the way towards an improved understanding of her responses to the world, as purposive ways of coping with her disorientation and altered perceptions. Her agency and self-expression are not limited or predetermined by the expectations of others, but instead, become an open possibility.

Case study

A woman in a care home with dementia refuses to come out of her room or eat, and hears several voices that she describes as 'gangsters'. She becomes very agitated, distressed and aggressive whenever care staff enter her room and attempt to provide any personal care. On further investigation, it turns out that the voices correspond to those of a group of drug-dealing youths who lived in the flat above where she used to live. They had caused a fire which forced her out of her flat. In her reality, the care staff have become the youths.

[Taken from a case study provided to the inquiry What is Truth? Truth and Lying in Dementia Care published by the Mental Health Foundation, December 2016. Available at: www.mentalhealth.org.uk/publications/ what-truth-inquiry-about-truth-and-lying-dementia-care.]

2 Recognition of the person

The second feature of hermeneutic competence involves *recognition of the person*: namely the ability to see the other individual in her uniqueness, as a separate entity from oneself, with her own particular perspective and vantage point. The importance of individual selfhood seems enshrined in our Western cultural stand-point, yet our often poor understanding of impairment combined with power dynamics within relationships can eclipse this very important point. This leads to the harmful tendency to (1) *objectify* (treat as an object) and/or (2) *assimilate* (treat as a reflection of others) persons with impairments, effectively denying them their own personality and individuality. These tendencies emerge, not just at a societal level, but also in the daily interactions within their circle of support, and thereby need to be proactively resisted.

When persons are treated as an object, they are essentially denied their subjectivity – they are no longer viewed as 'subjects' who have their own views and perspective. Instead, they are used as a tool, an instrument, for our own purposes; we use them as a mere means to promote our own ends. The philosopher, Immanuel Kant, famously claimed that we fail to show proper respect to other persons when we treat them as an object in this way, because such treatment suggests that they don't have their own ends, desires, needs or views that are worth considering (see Appendix 4).

The harmful exploitation of a person's dependence on us for care, guidance and encouragement can cause this type of objecti-fication. For example, individuals with a learning impairment might be manipulated and told certain narratives about their helplessness and stupidity so they more readily comply with the wishes of their caretaker, or those with dementia may experience intimidation by family members in order to gain control over their money and estate, or those with impairment are given a 'Do not resuscitate order' without their consultation because their family members or clinicians presume these people have no preferences and views worth considering. Treating others as an object in this manner assumes that persons with impairment are incompetent, untrustworthy and passive bystanders to decisions that affect them; it invalidates their unique perspective and, indeed, presumes that they don't have one in the first place.

The second tendency is to assimilate persons with impairment, treating them as a mere reflection of others around them. In this case, we might acknowledge that these individuals *do* have their own point of view but *we presume to know and understand it even better than they understand it themselves*. We presume that *our* standpoint can represent that of others: our own views, desires, values and perceptions come to dominate the other person, so that she is no longer treated as a separate entity from ourselves. She is a mere extension of ourselves. In this way, her unique subjectivity is denied, much like when an individual is objectified.

Assimilation points to something slightly different from our normal connectedness: when we are in intimate relationships, for example, some degree of integration always exists. We might speak on behalf of our partner because we know that he doesn't like radishes, or she prefers to watch a film at home rather than go to a party. And when we speak on behalf of them we might legitimately say, 'Jane won't want to go to that party' or 'John will avoid the salad with radishes'. But assimilation goes beyond this, where we might *reject* Jane's protest that she would like to go to the party, and say 'I know what you *really* want. You want to stay at home.' The temptation to assimilate another's standpoint is all the stronger in cases where a person relies on others to convey her wishes and preferences on her behalf due to communicative challenges. For example, the parent of a person with a learning impairment might claim to speak for her son, even as behavioural cues, like sounds of distress, banging his head repetitively or self-harming, might indicate that these preferences are not his own. Or consider cases of relational enmeshment, where the needs of the caretaker are often imposed on another; the carer's desire to be needed and wanted is presumed to reflect the other's need for them to the point that the person with impairment is subject to an increasingly controlling regime of treatment and care.

Both objectification and assimilation exploit the unequal power dynamic in a way that harms and disrespects individuals. Depending on the level of impairment, a person can be more vulnerable to the type of care and treatment she receives from those within her circle of support. When persons with impairment are treated as objects or as mere reflections of myself, I misuse that power in a way that implies that these individuals are not separate from me, that they don't deserve to have a different perspective which *I could learn from*. Instead, I presume either that *I know best* or *I don't need to consider their views*. As a result, I not only fail to properly understand and recognise the person before me, but I fail to understand myself – *my* prejudices, *my* perceptions that make up *my* own standpoint which in fact, could be barriers to me understanding others better.

Recognition of the person will therefore mean I see the person before me as *separate* and *independent* from me, as a person whose unique needs, perspective and views are worthy of consideration. Importantly, I assume in the first instance merely the *possibility* of understanding better, not that I *will* understand the person. This is an important difference: think of cases where a person does or says something that is bewildering to you: it immediately seems like you are encountering something that is foreign and different. We can't presume to know the person's frame of reference in the first instance. To understand that person, we need to open ourselves up to the possibility of learning *how* and *why* this frame of reference may be a valid perspective that leads to an understandable way of reacting (see Appendix 3). I might presume to understand why a boy with autism is suddenly jumping – for instance, I presume it is because he wants to express joy, or he wants to annoy those around him. These explanations of his behaviour might make sense *to me* and allow me to explain to others how his behaviour is comprehensible. But this does nothing to properly recognise *him*, understand *him* and what jumping *means to him*. To learn that the boy jumping is in fact a way of releasing affective distress, I need to open myself up to seeing him as a distinct individual who is separate from me, acting from his own standpoint and a frame of reference that I might not initially know or share. Only then will I have the curiosity to find out more, and even hope to grasp and understand him. In other words, recognition of the person will always involve a delicate balance between connection and distance, between familiarity with and curiosity towards the unfamiliar.

Case study

A woman was one to whom the epithet 'conventional' could never be applied. By her own account, the account of her eldest daughters and the account of her father, she had led a life characterised by impulsive and self-centred decision-making without guilt or regret. She had had four marriages and a number of affairs and had spent the money of her husbands and lovers recklessly before moving on when things got difficult or the money ran out. She had, by their account, been an entirely reluctant and at times completely indifferent mother to her three caring daughters. Her consumption of alcohol had been excessive and, at times, out of control. She was, as all who knew her and she herself appeared to agree with, a person who sought to live life entirely and unapologetically on her own terms – that life revolving largely around her looks, men, material possessions and 'living the high life'. In particular, she had placed a significant premium on youth and beauty and on living a life that, in her words, 'sparkled'.

She was diagnosed with cancer, experienced a breakdown of a long-term relationship, financial difficulties and the prospect of arrest for an incident that occurred during the breakdown. She attempted suicide but did not die. In consequence, she needed life-saving treatment (renal dialysis). Without it, the almost inevitable outcome would be her death. Administering the treatment would be very likely to save her life, although there was an appreciable – and, with the passage of time, increasing – possibility that she would be left requiring dialysis for the rest of her life. The woman refused to consent to the dialysis and much of the treatment associated with it. To her, the prospect of growing old, the fear of living with fewer material possessions and the fear that she had lost and would not regain her 'sparkle' outweighed the potential that dialysis would save her life.

The medical team treating her considered that she did not have capacity to refuse the treatment, on the basis that she was unable to use and weigh the relevant information. They took the view that her inability to use and weigh the information was as a result of a personality disorder, although they accepted that it might also result from her stubbornness or bloody mindedness. Her family, and in particular her two elder daughters, supported her in her decision on the basis that she had capacity and gave evidence that her reasons for refusing treatment might not be easy to understand, but that they were 'not only fully thought through, but also entirely in keeping with both her (unusual) value system and her (unusual) personality'.

In finding that the woman had the capacity to refuse the treatment, the judge held that:

> C's decision is certainly one that does not accord with the expectations of many in society. Indeed, others in society may consider C's decision to be unreasonable, illogical or even immoral within the context of the sanctity accorded to life by society in general. None of this, however, is evidence of a lack of capacity. The court being satisfied that, in accordance with the provisions of the Mental Capacity Act 2005, C has capacity to decide whether or not to accept treatment, C is entitled to make her own decision on that question based on the things that are important to her, in keeping with her own personality and system of values and without conforming to society's

expectation of what constitutes the 'normal' decision in this situation (if such a thing exists). As a capacitous individual C is, in respect of her own body and mind, sovereign.

[Taken from the 39 Essex Chambers report of King's College NHS Trust v C & V [2015] EWCOP 80.]

3 Open dialogue and humility

Disputes in capacity adjudications and around best interests judgements often revolve precisely around difficulties in achieving some common understanding: practitioners can lack what is needed to engage in genuine dialogue with persons with impairment, meaning there could be unwarranted assumptions about their capacity to make decisions or their values and perspective. The third feature of hermeneutic competence therefore refers to the ways in which we can facilitate understanding and connection through open dialogue and humility: this enables us to be critically aware of our own prejudices and their effect – positive or negative – on our interpretation of the words and actions of those with impairments. Open dialogue simply means that we are receptive to what another tells us, that we listen carefully and with an open mind. This is, of course, part of it. But equally important is what comes *before that* – namely how we *prepare* to engage in open dialogue. A lack of attunement to impairment, and the inability to understand and recognise a person as a separate individual, often stem from barriers that exist *within ourselves*.

Being skilled at open dialogue means we need to cultivate the right orientation and interpretive standpoint on numerous levels, particularly if we are to guard against objectifying or assimilating the person with impairment. This requires three steps. First, we need to acknowledge that our own framework of understanding – our own perspective – is steeped in its own prejudices and assumptions. Importantly, having a prejudicial framework is not just unavoidable, it also isn't inherently bad or good.[3] Prejudices in

---

3   See the Appendix 3 for further discussion.

the first instance are 'prejudgements'; they are the raw material we work with prior to coming to a settled view on things. We necessarily start with our own prejudgements based on our background, through experiencing our culture, traditions, socio-economic status, relationships. These mediate our interactions with others and form the lens through which we see the world. For example, I might grow up in a culture where milk isn't taken in my coffee after 11 in the morning (in some parts of Italy, for example), and it is highly unusual for a cappuccino to be drunk in the afternoon. My prejudgement might be that this is a regular practice everywhere, until I encounter different practices as I travel around the world, and my prejudgement that 'milk cannot be taken in coffee after 11am' might change accordingly. Of course, prejudgements aren't always as benign as the coffee example. One could start with all sorts of negative prejudgements, like 'a person with autism is disruptive', 'individuals with dementia are always confused', or 'people with learning disabilities are dumb'. We will have more to say about how we challenge these types of prejudices below: but the important point is that *prior* to challenging these, one has to be *aware* of them in the first place, and this awareness depends on recognising that we *all* unavoidably start with prejudgements, preconceptions and presumptions. *We can't challenge our prejudices and develop more nuanced views if we assume that they aren't there in the first place.* Once we recognise this as a starting point – that we are situated within our own frames of reference – we start to acknowledge that others are likewise situated, within their own frames of reference. Ultimately, perfect objectivity, or a view from nowhere that is free from prejudice, is an illusion.

Second, just because we start with prejudices doesn't mean that these can't be altered or found to be wrong. Awareness of our own prejudices means that we need to view them as provisional and changeable, particularly when we have encounters with others that challenge them. Only when we critically reflect on how our prejudices can potentially function as barriers or walls can a deeper, more nuanced understanding of others emerge. To use the example above, those around the boy jumping out of the blue might immediately view this behaviour as bewildering – even more so if they learn that he has autism. His manner of communicating seems alien and incomprehensible, and their inclination might be to objectify him, or impose certain meanings about his behaviour onto him as we described above, or distance themselves (as is sadly typical when one has highly stigmatising prejudices about disability or disorder). Bridging the communicative gap requires those around him to identify the prejudice that frames his behaviour as alien to them (e.g., 'normal people do not jump out of the blue'; 'autism causes individuals to behave in strange ways'), *then* critically reflect on how these prejudices prevent them from understanding what this boy is trying to communicate and express. *In what ways* are my prejudices, my concepts and my beliefs about certain things, closing me off from this boy's perspective? We effectively 'test' our own prejudices, our frameworks of meaning, and our ways of understanding another when we are genuinely open in dialogue and receptive to the potential truth of what the other person has to communicate to us.

The third step – the ability to challenge and test one's own prejudice – demands the cultivation of humility. To be humble means that we don't presume that we know 'better' than others; it implies a critical awareness of our limitations and realistic measure of our abilities. It denotes being open to the possibility that we might be wrong, that our understanding of something could be enhanced and improved through the unique perspective of another. Humility is crucial because it offsets the asymmetrical power dynamic – and the impulse to exploit it – in cases where individuals' impairment makes them particularly vulnerable to the care, treatment and surrounding narratives provided by their circle of support. Moreover, humility facilitates critical reflection on our presumptions, prejudices and frames of reference, creating some distance from these so that we can actively test them and refine our own understanding of something.

Part of the reason why humility can be hard to cultivate is due to deeply embedded, harmful attitudes that suggest persons with impairment have little to teach those who care for them.

Despite best intentions, such an attitude can be an ongoing temptation in relationships where one party bears greater responsibility for the care and support of another, and especially where communication remains a challenge. Cases of abuse, manipulation and enmeshment attest to the dangers associated with a lack of humility in dealing with persons with impairments. Yet the reality is that such individuals can enrich the perspective of those within their circle of support in profound ways. In *Love's Labor*, the philosopher Eva Feder Kittay provides a touching account of raising her severely impaired daughter, Sesha. She describes how Sesha's diagnosis prompted a visceral sense of her own limitations and vulnerabilities, fundamentally challenging Kittay's assumptions about what made life meaningful:

> Sesha would never live a normal life. [...] But the worst fear was that her handicap [*sic*] involved her intellectual faculties. We, her parents, were intellectuals. I was committed to a life of the mind. Nothing mattered to me as much as to be able to reason, to reflect, to understand. This was the air I breathed. How was I to raise a daughter that would have no part of this? If my life took its meaning from thought, what kind of meaning would her life have? (Kittay 1999, p.150)

The daunting challenges and responsibilities in the face of another's vulnerabilities could have made Kittay more entrenched about her strongly held beliefs (e.g., that an intellectual life is more valuable than other non-intellectual forms of life), more arrogant about the supposed truth of her viewpoint, and inclined to dismiss or control her daughter. Instead, the humbling experience of caring for her daughter heightened Kittay's awareness of, not just the predicaments of impairment for Sesha, but also *her own* weaknesses and prejudgements. This enabled the removal of obstacles that initially prevented Kittay from recognising her daughter as an individual in her own right, a being who expressed her own unique personality and was capable of teaching profoundly important life lessons to those around her. Kittay describes this poignantly: '[w]e didn't yet realize how much [Sesha] would teach us, but we already knew that we had learned something. That which we believed we valued, what we – I – thought was at the center of humanity, the capacity for thought, for reason was not it, not it at all' (p.150).

When approached with humility and self-awareness, dialogue can cultivate a common understanding with a person whose experiences and perspective seems initially alien to us, so that we see the potential truth in her standpoint. Like Kittay's experience with Sesha, it has the potential to shift, improve and change our understanding of what is valuable in life, what makes us human, how bonds of connection are forged and maintained. In this respect, we can say that relationships involving those with impairments are *reciprocal* even as their circle of support may bear greater responsibility for their care and treatment. Sesha might not offer to her mother intellectual, philosophical exchange; she might require her mother to care for her in ways that she cannot return in kind. But she could offer irreplaceable acts of love, affection, companionship, emotional connection and, indeed, a unique perspective on human vulnerability, capacity and value.

Indeed, when open dialogue and humility run through the circle of support around the person with disabilities, this facilitates a unified, collaborative effort towards finding the best means of enabling decisional capacity. It is important to be mindful of how these traits of open dialogue and humility could be absent in relationships and practitioners should be prepared to act in some way, as we will discuss later in the book. Numerous cases show how easily conflict can emerge between family members, practitioners and assessors when different sides have fixed, trenchant ideas about what they believe to be best for the individual. The skills of open dialogue and humility can help ameliorate the dangers of an overly fixed view and cultivate mutual understanding for the enablement and respect of the person with impairment.

Case study

Mr B was a 73-year-old with a long-standing history of mental illness together with, in more recent years, poorly controlled type 2 diabetes. Mr B had for many years experienced persistent auditory hallucinations in which he heard the voices of angels and of the Virgin Mary. Although he did not consider himself to belong to any particular religion, he considered that Mary wished him to be a Catholic. After the death of his long-term partner in 2000, he had lived by himself for many years, as an isolated but not unsociable person with an interest in the outside world whose mental illness did not cause him undue distress.

Mr B developed a chronic foot ulcer that did not heal despite various interventions, resulting ultimately in his admission to hospital. He was in hospital for a sustained period of time, resisting medication for his diabetes and antibiotics for his foot. Ultimately, the case came to the Court of Protection for declarations and decisions as to Mr B's medical treatment and, specifically, for authority to the NHS Trust responsible for his care to carry out an amputation on his leg. It was clear from the evidence before the court that, in the position Mr B was now in, not carrying out an amputation would lead to Mr B succumbing to an overwhelming infection within a matter of days; conversely, his life expectancy if the operation was successful would (very tentatively) be in the order of around three years. One of the main reasons why Mr B refused the treatment was, as he told the judge, 'I know where I'm going. The angels have told me I am going to heaven. I have no regrets. It would be a better life than this.' The judge was asked to place less weight on his wishes and feelings as a matter of principle, as Mr B lacked capacity to make decisions as to his medical treatment. However, the judge refused, making clear that:

> In some cases, of which this is an example, the wishes and feelings, beliefs and values of a person with a mental illness can be of such long standing that they are an inextricable part of the person that he is. In this situation, I do not find it helpful to see the person as if he were a person in good

health who has been afflicted by illness. It is more real and more respectful to recognise him for who he is: a person with his own intrinsic beliefs and values. It is no more meaningful to think of Mr B without his illnesses and idiosyncratic beliefs than it is to speak of an unmusical Mozart.

The judge held that:

43. Mr B has had a hard life. Through no fault of his own, he has suffered in his mental health for half a century. He is a sociable man who has experienced repeated losses so that he has become isolated. He has no next of kin. No one has ever visited him in hospital and no one ever will. Yet he is a proud man who sees no reason to prefer the views of others to his own. His religious beliefs are deeply meaningful to him and do not deserve to be described as delusions; they are his faith and they are an intrinsic part of who he is. I would not define Mr B by reference to his mental illness or his religious beliefs. Rather, his core quality is his 'fierce independence', and it is this that is now, as he sees it, under attack.

44. Mr B is on any view in the later stages of his life. His fortitude in the face of death, however he has come by it, would be the envy of many people in better mental health. He has gained the respect of those who are currently nursing him.

45. I am quite sure that it would not be in Mr B's best interests to take away his little remaining independence and dignity in order to replace it with a future for which he understandably has no appetite and which could only be achieved after a traumatic and uncertain struggle that he and no one else would have to endure. There is a difference between fighting on someone's behalf and just fighting them. Enforcing treatment in this case would surely be the latter.

[Taken from the 39 Essex Chambers report of Wye Valley NHS Trust v B [2015] EWCOP 60.]

Summary

Relationships can disable individuals' decision-making capacity; equally, their support can be a crucial factor in helping individuals realise their abilities to make choices in their lives and to carry them through. The very nature of the functional test of capacity tends to focus more on the competencies of the individual whose capacity is in question. However, accommodating how relationships affect capacity will shift this narrow focus towards the various abilities of those *around* persons with impairment. The features of hermeneutic competence, such as *attunement to the nature of individuals' impairment*, *respect and recognition of her unique personality and separateness*, and *openness to dialogue through humility*, will ensure those within the circle of support remain open to *the manner in which a person communicates* as well as *the message that she is trying to convey*. It is incumbent on those within the circle of support to cultivate such skills – the presence of impairment does not mean such individuals do not have their own unique perspective on things, their own framework through which they see the world. Together these skills of hermeneutic competence will help cultivate the right attitude of respect owed to persons with impairment. In the next chapter, we will look more specifically at the types of narratives that enable rather than disable decision-making capacity, and in the chapter that follows how the same sets of skills can help us when the line between capacity and best interests is crossed.

Checklist of reflective questions

- What makes you feel recognised as a person when you have a conversation others?

- When was the last time you felt understood and had a personal connection with a peer in a conversation? What was it about the conversation that made you feel understood and connected?

- When was the last time you revealed something personal to a peer? What was it about the conversation that made you feel safe to reveal it?

- When was the last time you were in a country or place where you did not speak the language or understand the customs? How did you try to communicate and adapt?

- Thinking about the answers to these questions, how would you like the person deciding your fate to engage with you?

- What is the first word that comes to your mind when you think of 'disability'? 'Impairment'? 'Support'? What prejudices do these reveal? How are these prejudices positive or negative?

- Can you give an example of when you may have *objectified* and *assimilated* someone, or someone objectifying or assimilating you? How do you think it felt to the other person? How did it feel to you?

- What kinds of experiences and interactions with others have you found humbling? How can humility become part of daily professional life in interacting with individuals with impairments?

Chapter 4

Enabling and Disabling Narratives

The importance of narratives

In the film *Sliding Doors*, two parallel life stories unfold depending on whether or not the main character, Helen, misses or takes a particular journey home. In one chain of events, Helen discovers her cheating partner, leaves him and goes on to find a new love and start her own company. In the other, Helen doesn't discover her partner's infidelity and struggles unhappily, supporting the two of them with a couple of part-time jobs. The basic premise of this film is that the combination of random circumstance and choice can lead to drastically different realities for a person.

The narratives and stories that run through our lives reflect a similar dynamic between unchosen circumstance and the subsequent choices we make. A person doesn't choose what family she is born into, what stories she inherits, or the narratives of others. If she is consistently told she is stupid, worthless and helpless, this will influence how she views herself and the choices she makes accordingly; equally, the same person who in opposite circumstances is told she is valued, trustworthy and able is likely to lead quite a different life. Surrounding narratives and stories can have a profound effect on how we understand and define ourselves; they effectively become part of our *own self-narratives* – the stories we internalise and tell ourselves to help make sense of our choices. They help inform the direction of our lives.

The unique perceptual and cognitive challenges among those with impairments amplify the importance of surrounding narratives, particularly in addressing the 'predicaments' of impairment discussed in the previous chapter. Disabling narratives can render these predicaments as fundamentally negative, undesirable and unacceptable – essentially reducing individuals to their bodily features of impairment and hampering their ability to make decisions. Equally, narratives have the power to enable, encouraging self-acceptance and autonomy regardless of the predicaments of impairment. In this chapter, we ask the question: How can practitioners (1) distinguish between narratives that are enabling or disabling and (2) ensure that they consciously engage in narrative practices that encourage and empower a person's decision-making abilities? We suggest that practitioners should be attuned to how harmful stigmatising views about impairment often underlie disabling narratives. Moreover, this chapter explores how certain kinds of narratives are conducive to authentic self-expression and autonomy. This helps set up the next chapter, where we will examine what practitioners can do in cases where disabling narratives have incapacitated individuals with impairments.

Stigma and disability

Negative, disabling narratives are often caused by stigmatising attitudes and views about persons with impairment. Stigma can be defined as the adverse or punitive response to a perceived negative trait among individuals or groups (Goffman 1963). Earlier in the book we discussed how all of us begin with prejudices of some kind. Stigma emerges mainly from unchallenged negative prejudices about socially undesirable differences. This in turn leads to a variety of adverse responses, such as:

- reducing individuals to their (undesirable) traits

- isolating them because of these traits

- repeating discriminatory narratives about such difference.

Crucially, stigma is *relational* and *social*: it emerges, not as an intrinsic attribute of individuals, but *through social interaction* and *inequalities in power.* It is revealing that one of the earliest uses of the term was in connection with the markings given to slaves – seen as somehow less than human. The comparative social power and status of those without impairments has meant the ideal of the person 'sound in mind and body' is seen as 'normal'. Because persons with impairments apparently deviate from this standard, they lack or lose status in their communities, preventing them from participating fully in social, economic and political life, and further disempowering their abilities to counter these pernicious, negative views about difference.

Stigmatising practices are everywhere, from the portrayal of disabilities in the media to the way in which those around the individual with impairments address her or the language that they use in her presence to describe her. The more invisible harms of stigma lie in its denial of the social recognition, acceptance and belonging we all need to flourish. For example, an ethnographic study by Jahoda and colleagues powerfully describes the importance of social recognition for those with intellectual impairments (Jahoda *et al.* 2010). One of the participants, Gary, expressed his sense of isolation and frustration when trying to gain acceptance among his peers. The community nurse described Gary as:

> want[ing] to be part of mainstream (society) but because of his disabilities he's unable to make that gap (*sic*) and he doesn't see himself as being disabled – he doesn't go to anything that's really obviously a disabled group...he's trying to be part of what everyone else does really (p.527).

Gary's desire for social acceptance and status was further chronicled in a photo series of an evening out: at face value, he looked to be part of to be part of a crowd of young men and women. Yet on discussion, Gary revealed that he knew almost none of the individuals in the photographs. Moreover:

> [t]he final three photographs show[ed] him being taken to the accident and emergency unit of a local hospital by a policeman, after trying to throw himself in front of a car at the end of the night. This followed an incident at the end of the evening when

he had tried to speak to a girl, and this led to him being spat on by her boyfriend and his friends (p.527).

Obviously, this example shows that stigma can be experienced explicitly through abuse, physical assault or verbal insults (like when one is called 'handicapped' or 'crippled' to purposefully demean and exclude). But equally pernicious is the stigma that is implicitly felt and absorbed at a perceptual and emotional level. Stigma isn't just a societal and structural problem, but can manifest itself within the circle of support, where individuals with impairments are isolated, feared or infantilised by those around them. In these cases, distance and separation are felt through everyday relationships and interactions, like Gary comparing himself to others without impairments, perhaps even denying and rejecting features of himself in an effort to be more like them. Insight into the specific nature of one's impairment, or the ability to 'name' one's disability isn't necessary to feel stigmatised in this manner. The effect is nonetheless the same: whether at the level of relationships, broader society, or structural barriers, stigma often relegates those with impairments to passive, child-like individuals to be pitied or acted on, leading to the deprivation of opportunities and the suppression of autonomy by well-intentioned but overprotective parties or policies. Or they are viewed as invisible, incapable of knowing and acting on their own mind and subsequently excluded from developing a shared meaning of the world with others to establish some common understanding. Or in cases where impairment may be 'invisible', stigma could cause individuals to be blamed for their deviance, so they are viewed as problematic persons requiring management, particularly prior to their condition being medically 'labelled' or diagnosed.

The more worrying aspect of stigma is how these pernicious narratives that equate 'normal' with 'able-bodied' develop an air of objectivity and truth, not just for society, but for *individuals with impairment*, to the point that it fundamentally damages their personal identity. Green *et al.* (2005) describe the case of Homer whose personal identity was intimately connected with his role as a US Marine officer. However, he gave up his career once he had acquired a physical impairment, not because others pressured him to do so, but because of the stigmatising views about disability he had internalised. Homer described:

> I don't think they thought less of me, but Marines expect their leaders to be able to lead. … Even though I could do it in garrison…it was obvious that…if we had to go into combat, that I could possibly let them down. … That impacts them whether or not they ever say anything (and they never did). …I know as a Marine, when you have a leader who cannot do everything he knows he is supposed to be able to do…it affects the unit. … I would like to think that I was a Marine 110 percent of my life. … So as a Marine officer, knowing that I couldn't do the things I should do to be a leader, to be a Marine, that had a significant impact…on my self-esteem. … So that's how I came to be retired from the Marines (p.207).

Our identities are formed through the contributions of different perspectives over time, and these can be severely challenged with the onset of an impairment (as in Homer's case), or when we feel we are *abnormal*, or *less than the ideal*, simply by absorbing the norms about able-bodiedness around us. The philosopher Hegel (1977) describes how individual consciousness develops when others acknowledge our existence: in simple terms, we develop our identity through the lens of others. This *process of mutual recognition* describes how our identity and sense of self is formed through interpersonal interaction (see Figure 4.1). The social status that is accorded to us by others – how they view and treat us in interpersonal interactions – becomes internalised and mimicked within ourselves. We utilise it as a template for how we understand, describe and treat ourselves. Stigmatising experiences like Gary's night out or the underlying culture of the Marines for Homer may in fact describe *mis*-recognition, which can lead to ways of viewing and defining ourselves that can be contrary to autonomy. When we are viewed through stigmatising lens, we might start to *believe* that we are lesser or different in a bad way, which impacts on our choices accordingly.

But proper recognition of the person, like we described in the previous chapter, can be a corrective to stigma. Stigma has two impulses: it picks out differences and deviations from a societal norm, then lumps together all individuals with these deviations into the same category. Mutual recognition challenges both of these impulses because it *starts* with the presumption that other selves *are* different and separate from ourselves, with their own unique needs and perspectives. *Only once this difference is acknowledged is it possible for us to come to a closer understanding of another person's perspective.* As we saw in Chapter 3, recognition of the person helps those within the circle of support achieve the delicate balance between connection and distance that is so vital for nurturing the autonomy of individuals with impairments. When we experience true recognition, stigmatising assumptions about difference and sameness are displaced, allowing authentic personal identity to be given space and encouragement to grow.

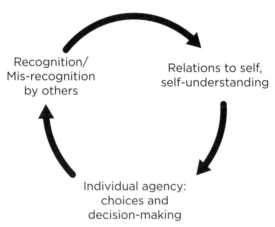

Figure 4.1: The cycle of mutual recognition

Case study

A man walks into a room full of doctors, gathered to receive training on the Mental Capacity Act. He has cerebral palsy and is to take part in a play as part of the training put on by a group with a range of impairments. Many of the doctors shift somewhat uncomfortably in their seats at the prospect of an hour of 'politically correct' theatre. They look even more uncomfortable when his opening words are 'I have a serious problem...' His next words change the rest of the hour. They are 'I am a Newcastle United fan.' Those six words enable the doctors in the room to see the man, not as a 'representative' of those with an impairment or cerebral palsy, but as a unique individual who has common interests with others in the room. One doctor even asks the man what he thought of the game on Saturday.

[Drawn from personal experience of one of the authors of the work (ARK) of the Twisting Ducks theatre company: http://thetwistingducks.co.uk]

Stories and counter-stories

Recognition or mis-recognition occurs through the narratives and stories that help shape our personal identity. Stories *depict* something about experience, *select* and *interpret* the relevant content and *connect* events, actions and characters to make sense of what is being represented (Lindemann Nelson 2001). Stories and narrative are essential to personal identity. 'Through one's own and others' selective, interpretive, and connective representations of the characteristics, acts, experiences, roles, relationships, and communities that contribute importantly to one's life over time, an identity makes a certain sort of sense of who one is. It does so because it is essentially narrative in nature' (Lindemann Nelson 2001, p.15).

Stories and narratives are important because they help us make sense of ourselves and the world around us; they help clarify why some values are significant to us and how these guide our choices.[1] But even more importantly, my own narratives

---

1   Narratives in the context of our discussion must be understood more expansively, to go beyond verbal dialogue or literacy skills to include other creative forms of self-expression, such as pictures, videos and photographs so that the alternative ways in which persons with impairments might express their personal identity and social belonging are taken into account.

and stories reflect the *content* of those which are communicated to me by my circle of support. As Lindemann Nelson writes, '[w]ho we can be is often a matter of who others take us to be. […] Your identity as a competent adult crucially depends on others' recognizing you as such' (p.81). If I am constantly told I am a competent person, that I have reason to be sure of myself, this will likely be how I represent myself to the world – I too will have reason to believe in my competence and see this as part of my personal identity. Enabling narratives within our circle of support thus help construct our identity as autonomous individuals because we emulate and internalise them in *nurturing relations-to-self: ways of engaging with our self as a person of value, worth, and deserving of consideration.* Nurturing relations-to-self are developed when others reinforce through narratives and stories that we are persons worthy of respect, trust and esteem; we in turn internalise these as ways we ought to treat ourselves, in order that (1) self-respect; (2) self-trust; and (3) self-esteem become part of our personal identity (see Figure 4.2).

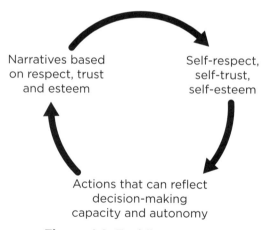

Narratives based on respect, trust and esteem

Self-respect, self-trust, self-esteem

Actions that can reflect decision-making capacity and autonomy

Figure 4.2: Enabling narratives

1 Narratives of respect

When others recognise the dignity of individuals – in terms of their social and legal identity – this can become internalised as *self-respect*. Self-respect implies that a person has a sense of her dignity and status, so that she sees herself as possessing personal authority and deserving of consideration. This can come in the form of formal legal rights. Perhaps the most profound importance of the CRPD lies precisely in the recognition that individuals with disabilities ought to have the status of *legal persons* and be treated as such. Underlying the Convention is a narrative of respect which suggests that the bodily and emotional integrity of persons with disability deserves equal consideration by others, as does their ability to deliberate and decide for themselves on matters that affect them. Narratives of respect can include the abstract, formal recognition of legal rights: for example, at the heart of the CRPD is the obligation of state signatories to 'ensure and promote the full realization of all human rights and fundamental freedoms for all persons with disabilities without discrimination of any kind on the basis of disability' (Art. 4.1), including the much discussed provisions of equal participation before the law in Article 12 and the recognition of legal capacity. But equally, small interactions within a person's circle of support can reflect narratives of respect, like when a practitioner provides privacy for a woman with Down syndrome to change her clothes or when family members ask rather than assume her views and preferences about where to live, ensuring their dialogue with her lacks a patronising or dismissive air. Such respect helps individuals adopt a similar disposition towards themselves so they understand themselves as deserving of equal treatment by others, recognising that their physical integrity, emotional life and reasons for their decisions warrant the due consideration of others.

By contrast, narratives of disrespect manifest themselves in numerous ways. It might be through the systematic refusal of legal rights and status for a group based on aspects of their identity, like physical difference, gender or race. The lack of legal status for individuals with disabilities can therefore engender a kind of societal disrespect which fuels stigma. The language of legal rights is undeniably a powerful tool to express the respect that is owed to us by others. Even so, we want to avoid making respect equivalent to *having rights* because someone could still be the recipient of disrespectful narratives even as her rights are formally secured, and vice versa. For instance, a person who may not enjoy a right can still be shown respect, like the Alzheimer's patient who might not (because of her current functional capacity) have the right to sign a binding financial contract but instead relies on an attorney who consults with her and genuinely cares for her well-being. Disrespectful, degrading narratives can occur at the level of everyday, mundane interactions, exercising a more invisible but highly damaging effect on the person's identity, where the arbitrary disregard of others is tolerated and accepted because she views herself as unworthy of respect (see Figure 4.3).

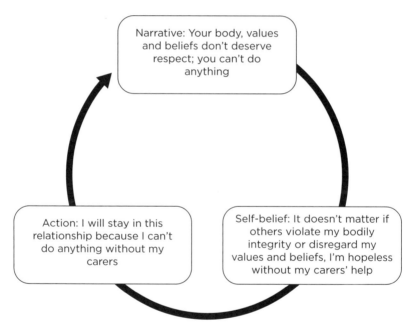

Figure 4.3: Example of a disabling narrative

Case study

A young man with mild learning disability was moved regularly around Europe and the UK by his mother. When they came to the attention of the authorities, the mother worked in hotels during the day, and told him that he was unable to leave the room in their accommodation because otherwise their bags would be stolen. He spent the day crouched by the door, waiting for his mother to return and feed him with the food that she had taken from the hotels where she worked. Because of the joint effect of his mild learning disability and the way in which he had been treated by his mother, he did not have any belief that he was an individual who was capable of making his own choices, but thought that he simply had to obey her. Removed, ultimately, from his mother's influence and placed in an environment where he was encouraged to understand that he had the ability and the right to make choices, he decided that he would like to see his mother from time to time, as he loved her, but that he did not want to live with her and would prefer to live in a place where, above all, he could study dinosaurs and visit the Natural History Museum.

(Taken from Re MP; LBH v GP [2009] Claim No: FD08P01058.)

2 Narratives of trust

Narratives of trust cultivate openness and faith in the more perceptual and emotional parts of how we see the world. These facets of our agency form a crucial part of the type of absorbed coping we discussed earlier in the book. Narratives of trust help validate our coping responses, where our perceptions and emotions are trusted to provide us with accurate, reliable cues about our context and environment. This enables the acceptance and exploration of our inner lives, cultivating a *self-trust* that is vital for the kind of self-reflection and authentic exploration needed for personal autonomy. When narratives of trust are absent – when our relationships shut down or question our emotional, perceptual responses to the surrounding environment – our coping responses change accordingly. It can lead to uncertainty that we genuinely feel a certain way or that our perceptions of something are accurate. For example, imagine that an overbearing father forbids his daughter with a learning disability from crying, especially when other kids tease and bully her. When she tries to explain why she feels sad, he adopts a dismissive attitude, accusing her of making a big deal out of nothing or telling her that she needs to toughen up to get by in this world. The next time she experiences the same hurtful remarks by others, she suppresses her emotional reaction instead of trusting that these might be understandable and appropriate responses to the situation. Even as she might accurately perceive the injustice of her treatment, she can no longer trust that her perceptual and emotional reading of the world is accurate. In the face of narratives of distrust, we constantly second-guess ourselves or gravitate towards the one response that is deemed acceptable by those around us. Or we replace our authentic feelings, perceptions and coping responses, with those of others because we mistake them for our own. We can't trust that our responses and perceptions are true, and we therefore don't engage in any reflection and exploration of this crucial part of our agency.

Case study

A young woman with learning disabilities and epilepsy has regularly been given injections of anti-epilepsy medication, and has been given them since childhood. She finds the injections painful, but she has learned that she should not complain, and should simply offer her arm for the injection, with her parents ignoring her pain and withholding her favourite doll early on if she failed to comply. Because she has learned to mask the pain effectively, everyone assumes that she is consenting to the injection, where in fact, her quietly enduring the injections is because she perceives that her feelings are not valid to those around her. No one stops to take the time to investigate with her what alternative ways of taking the medication might be better for her.

3 Narratives of esteem

We all need to feel as if we belong *somewhere*, where our activities and even our presence are viewed as valuable contributions to our surrounding community. Narratives of esteem communicate to us that we are important participants in communal rituals or patterns of living. This in turn develops *self-esteem* – where we imbue our activities with a similar esteem, believing in our positive contributions to those around us. A person matters, not because they are 'a son', 'a daughter', 'a friend', but because they are '*my* son, '*my* daughter', '*my* friend'. Consider collective projects like a community garden: a person who has certain impairments might struggle to understand the purpose of mulch, or planning the overall planting scheme for the garden, but she can sort out the compost, rake the leaves and rinse pots that are needed for plants. When those around her treat her contributions as important, they convey to her a sense of belonging within the community garden. In turn, she comes to see herself as a valued member of that garden – she sees her activities contributing meaningfully to the collective aims of the group. Moreover, narratives of esteem nurture the emotional well-being and sense of self-belief that fosters a healthy dynamic between connection and individual separateness needed for personal autonomy. This doesn't require some abstract reflection but could be internalised as a feeling or general intuition. Because the community gardener feels valued by and connected with others, she can better situate and understand her activities and goals: her *own* actions – whether it be washing garden pots, sorting the compost, raking the leaves – become imbued with a sense of personal and collective purpose.

When narratives of esteem are absent, a person might remain confused about her specific role within the community around her. Her activities become diminished and meaningless through her own eyes. Think of Gary in the example above: he seeks belonging with his peers and community, and we might well imagine the confusion and devaluation of self that develops when he is beaten up and rejected by others, when his efforts to belong are scorned and minimised. A sense of displacement dominates when our actions and we as persons are devalued; we struggle to situate our activities within a context of social meaning and significance.

The importance of narratives of esteem cannot be minimised in the context of our discussion. Practitioners consistently face difficult dilemmas around whether individuals should be put in long-term care as opposed to remaining in the home they share with their family or others close to them. Quite understandably, a practitioner's instinct is often to protect a person's physical and medical well-being, but we need to be mindful that these needs should not always be prioritised over the meeting of emotional needs, which include the esteem that comes from belonging somewhere, where one's presence *matters* to surrounding others. Regardless of how inclusive an institutional setting might be, it might be the case that the type of self-esteem that promotes autonomous agency and capacitious decision-making is through living within a community and place where one's contribution to different patterns of living is valued.

Case study

A young girl with Rett syndrome is wheelchair bound with Halloween coming up. Her siblings and cousins plan to dress up to go trick-or-treating together. Her parents take active steps to include her in all family activities, dressing up her wheelchair as a prehistoric car from the Flintstones and making a costume for her, so that she is included in the trick-or-treating with her siblings and cousins. Her family view her involvement as important, where something would be missing if she were not there to share these festivities with them.

Implications for practitioners

To summarise thus far, what we have suggested is that narratives of respect, trust and esteem help cultivate *nurturing relations-to-self*. These narratives frame and situate our own ways of understanding ourselves, encouraging the ability to make authentic and autonomous decisions that reflect a certain way of valuing ourselves. In other words, the narratives we tell ourselves, to make sense of our choices and actions and to understand who we are, will reflect the internalisation of surrounding narratives, whether these be of respect or disrespect, trust or distrust, esteem or disdain.

However, this isn't as simple as it appears for three reasons. First, narratives at the more personal level can worsen or alleviate disrespect felt at a more abstract, systemic level. A person with impairment might experience disrespectful narratives at a societal and legal level, but might nonetheless have a strong sense of her worth because her circle of support actively communicates narratives that counter this view. A disability rights activist might feel the narratives of systemic disrespect acutely, but her struggle against the injustice could be strengthened and validated by encouraging, respectful narratives by close family members and other persons with impairments supportive of the cause. This doesn't mean that narratives of disablement don't harm, injure and affect our sense of self. But it is a multi-layered picture.

Second, the function of stories and narratives in the context of disability is not always straightforward. Green *et al.* (2005) describe how close family members of a person with impairment, or indeed, the person herself, will repeatedly tell 'the stories of their lives' to health and social care practitioners. The manner of telling this story, the way that they convey it, could have profound implications on whether someone is given a diagnostic label of some kind and the treatment and attitudes of practitioners. These stories will often form the basis of professional judgements that are hard to remove from official case records. For example, consider the controversial diagnostic label, 'borderline personality disorder': a self-harming young woman with previous experience in psychiatric care may not wish to have this diagnostic label, and it can affect the story she conveys to the practitioners treating her. In fact, many patients have sought to fight the diagnosis on their official records, but this can be almost impossible to do. On acquiring this diagnosis, this young woman might find a change in attitude and treatment by practitioners, based on stigmatising, negative views about the diagnosis. As a result, someone who has been in and out of professional care, and her family who has lived through this experience, will often become very careful of and adept in how she presents herself (Green *et al.* 2005). We are most certainly not suggesting that practitioners invalidate these narratives on this basis, but rather wish to highlight the subtle and complex ways that stigma can affect the narratives of individuals with impairments: it can make someone feel more hesitant to disclose things about herself, it could make individuals fearful of being judged, and it could lead to being selective about expressing their feelings, views and perspectives.

Finally, practitioners might worry that this focus on narratives and stories might be illegitimate in the context of capacity and best interests assessments. Is it really the role of social workers, mental health clinicians or legal professionals to attend to narratives to the depth with which we recommend? But narratives are key for two reasons: first, *they provide an important tool which helps one to understand and assess the enabling or disabling characteristics of a person's circle of support.* Many practitioners might understandably baulk at the prospect of 'judging' the circle of support around the individual with impairment, but this is ultimately done *by listening to how an individual speaks and understands herself* – a practice that is *already* part of good practice in capacity and best interests assessments. How individuals understand and relate to themselves has a narrative structure and mirrors the narratives of those around them. This means that in listening to a person's manner of communicating to the content of her stories and narratives, we are given a window into the enabling or disabling quality of the relationships around her. Not all narratives are equal in our view: some reflect self-hatred, self-doubt or poor self-esteem. It is hard to provide any case for when these narratives are ethically *desirable or acceptable.* On that basis, the criteria of respect, trust and esteem seem reasonable standards to uphold, and practitioners in certain situations unavoidably make some judgements about the types of narratives that actively support or disable a person's agency, particularly if they are to treat the person in a manner that promotes her autonomy skills.

Second, narratives draw attention to *the dual function of practitioners within a person's circle of support*. Practitioners support individuals with impairments in a variety of ways, whether in facilitating pragmatic things like housing and treatment or encouraging participation in community activities and resources, like educational opportunities, or providing legal advice. Equally, this might mean taking a step backwards to assess whether that same circle of support is doing a sufficiently good job – including reflecting on *one's own* interaction with the person at the centre of this circle. This dual function means that practitioners have the potential to *identify* instances where the narratives need to change (to help challenge destructive, disabling self-narratives) and even *initiate and participate in* that process of narrative repair (to help cultivate more nurturing relations-to-self within individuals). More details about this reparative potential of practitioners will be discussed in the next chapter, where we explore the ethical role of the capacity and best interests assessor.

Summary

In this chapter we have suggested that practitioners need to consider how individuals' sense of themselves can reflect the enabling or disabling narratives that they have absorbed from those around them within their circle of support. When diminishing, denigrating narratives dominate persons' sense of themselves, it affects the very core of their personal identity. These can damage a person's agency and affect, not just the *process* by which a person decides, but also the *range of choices* that one envisages. This is true of us all, whether or not we have impairments. Nonetheless, the unique perceptual and cognitive challenges among those with impairment amplify the necessity for narratives and stories that emanate respect, trust and esteem, as well as challenge debilitating stigma, especially if our aim is promote decision-making agency. These criteria will help capacity and best interests assessors determine whether or not the person's circle of support helps foster or hinder autonomy. Context-specific, context-sensitive responses will be needed in scenarios where incapacitating narratives persist, as we will discuss in the next chapter.

Checklist of reflective questions

- When was the last time you felt excluded or judged by someone else based on your characteristics? What were the subtle and not to subtle clues that you were being excluded or judged? How did it feel?

- What specific stories and narratives have made you who you are? What has helped make you feel respected, trusted and esteemed? When have you felt the opposite? What role did others play?

- Do you find yourself 'tailoring' how you depict yourself to different people you are talking to? Are you being the 'real' you when you do so?

- Can you think of an example when you have encountered a family member, friend, work, colleague or stranger whose narratives gave you cause for concern for how they are being treated by others? Why did you find it worrying?

- What kinds of stigmatising beliefs and behaviours have you witnessed in your daily life and professional career? What strategies can you and other practitioners use to counter stigma against persons with impairment, even at a subconscious level?

Chapter 5

The Ethical Role of the Capacity and Best Interests Assessor

Introduction

Assessors at various levels, from the social worker meeting with a person on a daily basis to a Court of Protection judge adjudicating a case, can have an immense power over the lives of those with impairments. Because of this power, assessments can run into all sorts of dangers: individuals can feel inadvertently exploited, disrespected and powerless when this unequal dynamic between the assessor and assessed goes unchecked.

Practitioners as capacity and best interests assessors have an ethical role that is not often acknowledged, mainly due to the ideal of impartiality, which seems to define how respect for autonomy and equal treatment is often understood. Take the example of religion: the liberal state is referred to as an impartial entity that does not interfere on matters of personal faith or outwardly favour one religion over another, on grounds that citizens are to be treated as free and equal. Matters of personal conscience and faith, what they value and care about in their lives, are left for individuals to decide for themselves. In this context, practitioners understandably assume that any talk of their ethical role is shorthand for telling others what to do with their lives.

In this chapter we want to resist the common view that assessors are completely impartial agents. There is an undeniable ethical dimension to capacity and best interests assessment and this need not mean 'telling others what to do with their lives'. But it also doesn't suggest that sitting on the fence is a virtue either; indeed, sometimes practitioners have to engage with their deeper values and intuitions if they are going to carry out assessments in a manner that is respectful of and attuned to the person before them, not least so their *own* motives and reasons become more transparent.

So far we have explored the *relational* context of capacity and why it matters, such as ways in which narrative practices within the circle of support can encourage or impair a person's autonomy skills. Assessors aren't immune to this effect on the person. Assessments in and of themselves are interventions of *some kind* which can be carried out *ethically* or *unethically*: they can isolate the narrative damage done by others and help foster a person's agency; equally they can be disabling, stigmatising experiences that engender disempowerment and helplessness. Below we explore more fully the ethical function of capacity and best interests assessments by critically examining three areas: (1) the *presuppositions* of assessment; (2) the *interactions* of assessment; (3) the *reparative potential* of assessment. Reflecting on these three areas is important when we consider the particular dangers and problems within capacity and best interests assessments. We turn to these in the first instance.

When assessment goes wrong

Assessment may, on its face, seem relatively straightforward within the framework of the MCA. An assessor simply needs to ascertain whether or not the person is able to undertake the 'functional' requirements of decision-making, and then to ask whether any inability to do so is caused by a disturbance or impairment of the mind or brain (often determined by diagnosis). On the face of it, simple enough. Or in the case of best interests, assessors need to think of what is the objectively best course of action for the person. This naturally is a more complicated process, but through which the wording of s.4 of the Act helps guide the assessor.

Of course, assessment is not quite as simple as we have just made out, and there is a significant body of evidence that shows that assessors, at all levels, do not always find it easy to apply the provisions of the MCA (House of Lords Select Committee 2014). However, we do not want to focus here on the complexities of the law, but rather on the pitfalls that can emerge through the very fact of *being assessed* by another person. We highlight two here. First, an unequal power dynamic lies at the very heart of assessment – which can be exacerbated to the point of disrespecting the person with impairment when assessments are insensitively carried out. Second, where assessments might lead to quite drastic interventions into a person's life, there can be all sorts of underlying reasons for those interventions which may or may not be warranted, particularly when these reasons are inconsistent or couched in disabling language.

Power inequalities

We often forget that assessments of capacity and best interests are *themselves* interventions of some kind, and these interventions imply a particular power dynamic even if assessors have the right intentions. Many assessments come about when a person's choice diverges from the advice of professionals: for example, capacity becomes an issue when a woman with a learning disability refuses a recommended treatment for some physical ailment, or when an autistic young man wishes to remain in the home that his care team believes to be detrimental to his welfare. The fact that these individuals are defying the recommendations of practitioners is often seen as indication that their ability to make decisions might be impaired, or that their values and preferences should not carry weight in any best interests determinations.

Assessments – in particular assessments of capacity – could then be viewed as a disproportionate burden on those with impairments, even when they conclude *in favour* of an individual's choice. People take actions against the perceived wisdom of others all the time, some of which are personally harmful, whether it be eating or drinking too much on occasion or engaging in thrill-seeking activities that imperil their lives. But we don't assess the capacity of every person reaching for his third or fourth glass of wine or who goes free climbing.

By contrast, as soon as one has a diagnosis of some kind of learning or cognitive impairment, decisions that go against the perceived wisdom of professionals are questioned. Compare our reactions to the wine drinker or free climber with that of the example of an autistic man whose decision to stay in his home leads social workers to question his capacity. We might think that the problem ends when a judge arbitrates this disagreement and concludes that he *does* have the ability to decide where to live. But we sometimes fail to consider what impact this very process has on the person, *even if the assessment goes his way*. The very fact that someone is *being assessed* means that a person's life, his judgement, his manner of decision-making, is being evaluated based on some kind of doubt, implicitly communicating the message that we have reason to question whether something is the case. Doubt around his status as a *knower*, as someone who knows and understands what is right to him, can cause him to doubt himself or make him more distrustful of others.

Diagnosis and assessment can sometimes stack the cards against persons with impairment, and power inequalities can be exacerbated throughout this process if practitioners are not careful, amplifying another's sense of powerlessness, or worse, leaving them feeling disrespected and misunderstood. This could be when practitioners fail to properly listen and engage with what they are saying, remaining closed to their different perspective. It could be when assessors are unaware of the prejudices that frame their own way of approaching the individual and her context. It could be when assessors don't even speak to the actual person whose life they are affecting and fail to critically reflect on why this is the case. As we discussed in the previous chapter, individuals with impairments can be attuned to behavioural and environmental cues that communicate their exclusion and perceived difference.

Practitioners can have grounds to question whether a person has decision-making capacity, and they can justifiably both probe and intervene in certain cases. Indeed, *not* to do so could be just as harmful to the person's interests as to step back and 'hide behind' the presumption of capacity. Similarly, respect for the wishes and feelings of a person who has been found to lack capacity to make a decision does not always dictate that those wishes should be followed if there is a sufficiently strong countervailing reason. But an extremely delicate balance needs to be struck, where we check the presumption that the disproportionate power held by assessors is always appropriate and right, while considering what skills, what mode of communication, what competencies *on the part of the assessor* can help mitigate this inequality.

Case study

A local authority was concerned as to the influence that a live-in carer and her husband had over an elderly woman with dementia. Outwardly the woman seemed to be well cared for, her home was clean and tidy and she herself showed no physical outward signs of neglect or maltreatment. She was able to express herself and to communicate with people who visited and had been vocal in her appreciation of the care she had received. But she had been reported as complaining about the carer's care, of saying that she was restricted in what she was allowed to do in her own home, about what and when she was allowed to eat and drink and where and when she should sleep. She had expressed a fear of being placed in a care facility away from her home or being left in the care of the carer's husband, which she said she would find acutely embarrassing and unacceptable as she would not want her intimate needs met by a man. She was reported as saying that she had been threatened with both scenarios by the carer. At one point, she had described herself as being caught in a spider's web with the carer as the spider.

Conversely, she also made clear that she considered that she could make her own decisions without assistance and that she did not want anyone from the local authority or anywhere else sticking their nose into her life. Determination of her capacity to decide whether the carer and her husband should continue to live with her would determine whether it was *her* decision to make, or a decision to be made on her behalf by others.

This was a question which had to be answered, but answering in and of itself did count as interference: you may wish to read the case of *London Borough of Redbridge v G & Ors* [2014] EWCOP 485 (from which this case study is taken) and ask how well those asking and answering the question met the challenge.

Inconsistent justification

Practitioners can legitimately intervene in cases where those within the circle of support abuse, disable and fundamentally undermine a person's exercise of autonomy or agency. But as we will see, these interventions have to be sensitively carried out, with a clear sense of purpose and reasoning for them. In particular, the theme of this book is that there is a legitimate case for intervention where autonomy skills are not being fostered within a person's circle of care – by the same token, this means that practitioners have to be careful to ask whether these skills are being fostered or diminished.

The case for intervening might be relatively straightforward if a person indicates that this is what she would like, even if sometimes these indications may themselves be conflicted, reflecting the individual's own ambivalence or contradictory wishes. For instance, a young man with a learning disability might struggle to articulate the desire to leave the oppressive and abusive care of his mother, but nonetheless make clear that he would like to make his own choices. But what about the many cases where assessors have to consider intervening in a disabling relationship or care regime against the wishes of the person concerned? Practitioners might justify the intervention on grounds that it protects and promotes a person's autonomous agency, but what if that value isn't considered important to the actual person in those circumstances?

These relatively common situations can lead to *inconsistent justification*, the second potential pitfall within capacity and best interest assessments. Inconsistent justification applies when the reasons for intervention in fact replicate the disabling language, perceptions and circumstances which sanctioned intervention in the first place. For example, practitioners might consider intervening in the relationship and living arrangement between Nancy, a woman with mild dementia, and her abusive son. Despite her objections, her professional carers contemplate removing Nancy from the situation, as they see a marked deterioration of her physical, emotional and psychological condition and an increased dependency and fearfulness of others, coinciding with her son's presence in the house. She is increasingly isolated from others within her community. There is good evidence that her agency is likely to improve once removed from her son, expanding her circle of support to others who respect and value her. Assessors might have mixed views about whether or not Nancy has decision-making capacity, but take the view that her son's abusive treatment is a major factor in compromising that ability, such that intervention is in her best interests.

From our point of view, this reasoning in and of itself is not necessarily *ethically* problematic or questionable. But it is how assessors *rationalise* this course of action that matters. This is in part because of the way in which the test for capacity under the MCA is structured (to which we will return in Chapter 6). For present purposes, however, what concerns us here is the *ethical* basis of the reasoning.

Compare these two:

1. Though Nancy lacks capacity now, her autonomy and ability to decide are likely to improve within a more supportive and enabling environment.

2. Nancy lacks capacity now and even with a more supportive environment, she is unlikely to recover her capacity.

The ethical reasoning for intervening on the basis of (1) is much stronger than that of (2). The problem with (2) is the following. Sometimes assessments are unintentionally skewed in order to get the results that are wanted, leading to cases where a person's incapacity is used as a justification for why her views should be discounted, not just now, but even in future. An assessor might say an intervention is necessary to safeguard Nancy's autonomy and promote vital practical and social skills (and indeed, this often is the kind of reasoning behind removing individuals from disabling environments and relationships) but by the same token, deny that she is likely to regain capacity once removed from disabling circumstances. Why intervene then? How can we sanction safeguarding actions on the grounds of protecting her agency in the future, yet suggest that she is unlikely to ever recover her capacity to decide even in more supportive circumstances? By this reasoning, the very purpose of intervening is called into question. Indeed, this line of reasoning veers towards disrespecting the ability of persons with disabilities to decide on the types of relationships they wish to have.

Inconsistent justification also emerges in other ways, particularly where the language of assessment diverges from the empowering intent of the MCA. It can include dismissive attitudes towards a person's wishes and values, based on the presumption that she is helpless, incapable or unreasonable. It could be through the use of language that reinforces narratives of helplessness and incapacity (compare case studies 1 and 2 below). To really notice inconsistent justification requires greater awareness of the ethical perspective and orientation of the assessor, without which we fail to distinguish between the right and wrong kinds of interventions. Interventions then look like the paternalism that the MCA seeks to avoid, or worse, reflect the discriminatory treatment of those with impairments by those with more power.

Case study 1

A young man with autism is living in squalid conditions with his mother, who regularly denigrates and neglects him. Social workers are concerned with his isolation, physical and emotional health, and his extreme dependency on his mother. He lacks basic skills – not only does his mother not allow him to disagree or make decisions, but life and social skills for everyday living are completely absent. Social workers believe him to have potential to led develop these skills if he was removed from the care of his mother and given proper support. A best interests decision is made but ironically, certain assessors use *the mother's own disabling way of describing him* to justify their intervention (i.e., the environmental change might help but he is unlikely to gain capacity; he *might* develop some skills but his potential is quite limited in reality and he will remain helpless; the strength of his convictions must not be confused with capacity due to the impracticality of his wishes).

[Adapted from A Local Authority v WMA & Ors [2013] EWHC 2580 (COP).]

Case study 2

A young man with severe learning disability, developmental disorder, autism, epilepsy and diabetes was cared for at home and attended a day centre. His parents believed that he was unable to progress or develop new skills. Some professionals considered the staff's approach to the young man at the day centre as fundamentally flawed: a strategy where they would withdraw him from others to avoid outbursts was considered to leave the man isolated and understimulated, and served to reinforce his reliance on aggression. A new approach was proposed of an 'extinction burst', namely not to reduce stimuli causing the man's fight instinct to be aroused to seek to break the cycle between aggression and reduction of stimuli. This would be very painful and distressing to the man in the short term, both emotionally and physically. His parents were strongly opposed to the strategy, not least because they were afraid of what would happen if it did not succeed. The question was therefore whether it was in the man's best interests for him to be placed in a facility to undergo the 'extinction burst' approach: whether the temporary pain and distress was outweighed by the potential for long-term improvement in the man's abilities.

The court did find that the placement and approach was in the man's best interests, mainly to facilitate and enable the young man's potential beyond his current regime of care – acknowledging the love and commitment of his parents but also utilising his placement in the facility to foster strategies that would equip him better for independent living. The judge stated:

> There is no guarantee of success of course and I fully understand the parents' anxiety. I have been struck by how similar their concerns are to the fears of every parent whose child leaves home on the first steps to independent living. I don't intend in any way to trivialise the issues here by that observation nor to underestimate the impact of their bad experiences at [a previous placement]. I say it because the sheer normality of their reaction signals to me that [this man], like any other young man, is entitled to the opportunity to fulfil his potential; it is the opportunity and not the outcome that is his right. I would be failing to respect his personal integrity and autonomy if I did not afford him this chance.
>
> *[Taken from Re ML [2014] EWCOP 2.]*

The ethical function of assessment

The skills and abilities of assessors can help shape the boundary between appropriate and inappropriate interventions in the lives of those with impairments. Chapter 3 explored the importance of hermeneutic competence within a person's circle of support

– where practitioners and family members cultivate skills that recognise the unique individuality of the person and help interpret and understand her unique bodily coping and narratives. We also mentioned how these skills are vital to fostering the autonomy of others, where practitioners have a role to play in both judging and participating in the narratives that nurture positive ways of relating to the self.

This suggests that practitioners as assessors have an ethical role. One might baulk at this prospect, mainly because this seems to suggest that assessors are telling others what to do, perhaps treating individuals with impairments in a paternalistic manner. We tend to think of ethics as revolving around questions of how one should live, what is right and wrong, good and valuable. At first, it isn't quite clear how assessment – especially around capacity – would imply ethics. Social care workers, legal and medical professionals often think of capacity assessments as involving impartial, objective judgements. However, all sorts of presuppositions are involved in these assessments: about what it means to reason, about the information required for a particular decision, the risks and values of each option, and so on. All can and do impact on an assessor's perspective. Moreover, these presuppositions take on a particular lens depending on discipline: for example, legal practitioners will have their own lens framed by conventions in the law, just as social care workers will have a range of concerns and values framed by their own professional standards. Varied perspectives make it essential that capacity and best interests assessors are much more conscious of, and explicit about, the implicit assumptions which orientate these adjudications. These presuppositions are in many ways unavoidable, but practice needs to help make these more *transparent* so that the values and concepts revolving around capacity can be subject to further question and debate.

One barrier to this more transparent engagement with the ethical values and concepts around assessment is the common view of what it means to be a 'good professional'. We often think that upholding professional values means setting aside our own notions of what is ethical or good. These notions are subjective (applicable to individuals or specific groups) and possibly arbitrary, whereas professional values protect the fair treatment of people and avoid the imposition of one's personal values on another. For example, a nurse who is a devout Catholic might fundamentally believe that abortion is a moral wrong. But this belief cannot determine whether or not he cares for patients who do have an abortion. Being a good professional requires him to set aside his own personal belief system and ethical frameworks – these need to be *constrained* if he is to be a good clinician. Likewise, assessors are meant to apply the legal framework dispassionately, neutralising their own moral values. This holds even for best interests judgements that increasingly prioritise accommodating – or at least considering – the values of the person who has been found to lack capacity.

This separation between ethics and what assessors do as professionals is not only illusory, it also means we effectively conceal an important part of how practitioners themselves make decisions. We talk about the *values of the person receiving care and treatment*, but little is actually said about the values of the person doing the *assessing* or *judging*. The boundary between our ethical convictions and professional role can be quite difficult to establish, especially once we consider what is being looked at in capacity and best interests assessment, where one makes judgements about the nature of what it means to reason, what type of information is necessary to make a decision, how autonomy should be understood, and what 'best interests' mean.

To determine whether these values or judgements are warranted, we need to recognise that they are *there* in the first place, to engage with them in a transparent manner. This is the core starting point for developing hermeneutic competence. Part of the ethical function of assessors is to reflect on one's own values, not because these can legitimately override those of the person who is being assessed, but so that these can be *productive* and ensure that one's own orientation towards the individual is aligned with an ethos of empowerment and enablement. Ultimately, the ethical function of assessment becomes clearer when we critically reflect on three areas:

- The *presuppositions* of assessment: for example, what assumptions about reasoning, understanding and cognitive ability are contained within the functional test for capacity within the MCA.

- The *interactions* of assessment: for example, how assessment is carried out, whether participation and dialogue of individuals with impairment is encouraged.

- The *reparative potential* of assessment: for example, what assessors are uniquely placed to do when faced with situations of neglect, abuse and disablement within a person's circle of support.

The presuppositions of assessment

Three very common presuppositions demand further critical examination:

1. The assessor is 'outside' the circle of support of the person who is being assessed.

2. Practitioners should remain impartial and neutral during the assessment.

3. The functional pillars of capacity reflect relatively uncontroversial tests of intellectual and reasoning abilities.

Assumption 1: The assessor is 'outside' the circle of support of the person who is being assessed

This is true at one level: practitioners who are called on to assess a person's capacity or best interests might never have met the individual until the point of assessment. Indeed, assessment by nature has a more investigative purpose: to get relevant information, to examine the perspective of the person and reflect on the particular context and how it might bear on that person's decision-making abilities or where her best interests may lie. These interactions can be impersonal, brief and time specific, especially if the assessor has been appointed by the courts to arbitrate in a disagreement about capacity or best interests. Also, at least some assessments can be legally determinative in a way that, say a family member's observations might not be, suggesting that there must be at least a kernel of truth to this basic assumption. These factors together suggest that the 'outside' status of assessors can reflect immense power over individuals with impairment.

But being 'outside' the circle of support doesn't mean that assessors need not cultivate and exercise the same skills that are so crucial 'inside' that circle. This first demands an acknowledgement that interventions aren't confined just to the *outcome* of assessment, but include the *very process of being assessed*. Second, the hermeneutical competence we discussed earlier likewise needs to apply to assessors, not least to offset the dangers around power inequalities where assessors inadvertently become part of the *problem* of rather than *solution* to disablement. Skills of dialogue, recognising the person in her separateness, seeking to understand how a person understands herself through her narratives, sensitivity and genuine curiosity about a person's perspectives and values – these all are critical for assessors even within their investigative capacity.

**Assumption 2: Practitioners should remain
impartial and neutral during the assessment**

This common view is part and parcel of any professional training in social, legal and medical work, rooted in the importance of individual autonomy within our society. Respect for autonomy means those within a public (and indeed, private) capacity should avoid telling others how to live their lives and the choices they wish to make. This is especially important to persons with impairments who have often been historically the recipients of unwanted, unjustified and sometimes exploitative paternalistic care. So a stance of impartiality towards the individual's choices should be the aim in assessment, where one's own views and beliefs are left aside.

But some hidden dangers emerge when this assumption is adopted unreflectively. The claim that we can be completely neutral towards questions about ethical value, that we can somehow remove ourselves from the ethical frameworks that confer meaning to our actions, is not just naive, but fundamentally misguided. The concept of prejudice is vital here. As we discussed previously, one of the key insights of hermeneutics revolves around the acknowledgement of how our *own* prejudgements situate ways we understand and interpret others and the world around us. A 'view from nowhere' is not possible. If we presume that we can consciously and purposefully set aside our value frameworks and prejudgements at will, we risk denying how these bear on our interpretation of others and the world around us. But we don't simply acknowledge their existence and stop there: real hermeneutic competence demands that we prepare ourselves to be genuinely open to how our prejudgements might be challenged, how our viewpoint can be enriched through dialogue with others.

Assessors have to engage with their beliefs, their ethical views and their conceptual understanding. This isn't as unusual as we might think, but is in fact an essential part of numerous professional practices. Consider how judges assess end-of-life cases or situations of artificial nutrition: on the one hand, there are the legal principles within the law. But on the other, the values that society deems important – like the (sometimes overriding) importance of life – can impact on a judge's interpretation of the case. And indeed, this process of applying the law, judging and assessing the social context might challenge the prejudices that are embedded within particular interpretations of the law, especially when values in society change (see Hedley 2016).

The point here is that prejudice orients our outlook at multiple levels, informing:

- personal ethical views

- cultural and societal values

- professional values and frameworks.

These different levels aren't necessarily separate – for example, sanctity of life is a value that is enshrined in our social and cultural fabric, but it likewise influences our personal morality and the values that are upheld in certain professions (consider the vigorous and multi-layered debates around assisted dying). Some kind of bleeding between the different levels of values is inevitable, as are the multiple conflicts between them. Sanctity of life is a powerful ethical, societal and professional value, but so is personal autonomy. Sometimes arbitrating between these two is a case of trying to compare the incomparable. Indeed, at the heart of many disputes about capacity and best interests assessment is an underlying conflict about values – about which values are important and how the values of the assessor might conflict with that of the person under assessment.

We might say that this provides good reason why assessors ought to be neutral and impartial. But our point is that the ideal of neutrality often neglects the fact that we are all situated within some kind of value framework, with our own prejudgements. This doesn't mean they don't change. *But for them to change*, we need to acknowledge our own starting points, so that they become a productive platform for entering into dialogue with the person who is being assessed. Rather than uphold neutrality as the goal, assessment ideally ought to focus on *enriching* our respective value frameworks through this dialogue so as to develop a more nuanced understanding of the person undergoing assessment.

Assumption 3: The functional pillars of capacity reflect relatively uncontroversial tests of intellectual and reasoning abilities

A functional standard of capacity is often thought to be less discriminatory than outcome- or diagnostic-based tests. This makes sense intuitively: if capacity depended on assessors agreeing with the outcome or consequences of a choice, this would be paternalistic, while if capacity depended on the person's diagnosis, this would fundamentally discriminate against individuals with certain disorders. A functional test – at least on paper – appears to evaluate the most basic cognitive skills that are needed to make an informed decision, focusing on the *procedure* of decision-making rather than the actual *content* of one's decisions: the ability to understand core concepts around a decision, to compare and contrast the different options and their consequences, the ability to retain information and communicate one's decision.

But this focus on intellectual and reasoning abilities can embed all sorts of controversial assumptions, particularly in three areas. First are *assumptions about diagnosis and impairment.* The capacity of individuals with eating disorders is a good example here. Assumptions about diagnosis often affect the way that practitioners assess the functional pillars of capacity for the patient with anorexia nervosa (AN). On the one hand, AN patients can often pass functional-based competency tests test with flying colours: decisions to refuse treatment fulfil the various criteria of understanding, using and weighing information and so on, by their own internal logic (Tan *et al.* 2003). On the other hand, the patient's treatment refusal is often deemed incapacitous by appealing to the diagnosis: the person with this disorder cannot actually make a capacitous decision about food or treatment since AN by definition is the pathological fear of gaining weight and overwhelming value of thinness. This strategy is problematic and one may or may not agree with it (Kong 2014). But for present purposes, we simply want to make the point that assumptions about diagnosis and impairment can and do intrude on how functional abilities are interpreted.

Second are debatable *presuppositions about the various pillars of the functional test.* Reasoning abilities tend to be thought of as relatively uncontroversial – they involve the individual mind; they require the intellectual processing of information (like the ability to compare and contrast different alternatives); they use standards of consistency and coherence, not just so certain rules of logic are adhered to, but to ensure that rational deliberation is aligned with a person's values. However, these *are* in fact relatively controversial assumptions on several fronts, as illustrated in the following example. Consider a man with schizophrenia whose delusions involve hearing the voice of God which tells him not to take his medication. His reasoning appears internally consistent according to rules of logic; they even seem to reflect his own values ('God is telling me not to take my medication. I value my relationship with God. Therefore, I will not take my medication'). Yet, an assessor might actually judge his reasoning to be impaired *because* he is unable to adapt his reasoning to facts that are consensually held by those around him (that by refusing his medication he neglects his self-care to dangerous levels, becomes vulnerable to attack by others, or is in danger of losing his housing). The assessor perceives reasoning to involve, not just internal consistency, but the ability to adapt and respond to the facts within one's circumstances and environment.

Consistency is never just 'internal', but can involve a kind of to-and-fro interaction between ourselves and the facts and information provided by our external environment. None of us reasons or thinks in a vacuum. To what extent, then, is the functional test an assessment of our ability to interact with the facts, ideas and situational features around us? To what extent is there the presumption that some kind of consensual truth exists that our reasoning needs to take into account? Even then, sometimes the consensual truth isn't so 'consensual': assessors often make assumptions about the relevant content that needs to be understood, used and weighed in making decisions about, say, whether a person wants to live in independent living or get married. Some might hold the threshold quite high (e.g., the capacity to move into independent living requires understanding all the consequences of a tenancy agreement) or they might hold it quite low (e.g., capacity requires merely articulating what one wishes and the most basic consequences of moving into independent living, like remembering to turn off the stove). And whether or not a person is likely to be found to have capacity will depend on what content an assessor assumes to be necessary to 'use and weigh' or 'understand'.

Another controversial assumption is the singular focus on the *cognitive* rather than the *physical or emotional* aspects of decision-making. The ability to decide appears to reside purely in thinking things through logically, adopting a slightly detached perspective, which allows us to compare and contrast things without the disruptive influence of emotion, impulse or physical ways of coping. A kind of mind-body dualism casts a formidable spell within our culture, along with biomedical models of disorder and illness, where the authentic sense of self and higher order abilities are thought to reside in the mind rather than the physical body and its impulses.

But this cognitive bias in the functional test is deeply problematic, for reasons forcefully explained by Mark Neary in a revealing guest blog on the *Adult Principal Social Worker Network* (2017) about navigating the MCA with his autistic adult son, Steven. Mark talks of 'idiosyncratic Steven outcomes' in these capacity assessments, one of which revolved around Steven's ability to decide where to live. In Mark's words:

> No matter that several times a day, [Steven] would say to whoever was listening that he wanted to go back home. No matter that he would greet the manager of the unit every morning by singing Queen's 'I Want To Break Free'. And no matter that Steven escaped from the unit several times while he was there and tried to find his way back home. None of this counted as a gauge of his capacity and one day we attended an appointment with an assessing psychiatrist. All went swimmingly and no matter how each question was phrased, Steven was able to say that he wanted to live in the Uxbridge house (his home). (2017)

When Mark tried to assist Steven with how to interpret a comparative question – because Steven was confused by the word 'better' – he was asked to leave, and Steven was then found to lack capacity. Steven likewise failed to pass the capacity assessment to determine his ability to manage a tenancy, where talk of tenants and rent with had resonated strongly with Steven's liking for the Pet Shop Boys. These experiences left his father with the following view:

> I feel the mental capacity assessment in itself can be discriminating towards the disabled person. The very nature of the assessment means that the person has to demonstrate that they can take a piece of information, absorb it, weigh up the pros and cons and then come to a decision. It is a purely, cognitive, head-centred piece of work. Yet for the non-learning disabled person, we are allowed to use other organs of our bodies when making a decision. How many people have made a decision purely based on what our heart is telling us to do? How many of us rely on our gut instinct to inform our decision-making process? Neither of those very valuable containers of information is afforded to the learning disabled person during a mental capacity assessment. ... Already disadvantaged, they are expected to show a mental process that others would never have to do. (2017)

These words express powerfully the ramifications of having an overly cognitive account of the functional test. People with impairments are treated differently, held to a different standard. It could mean that a person's very understandable frustration with being assessed or institutionalised is somehow read as *evidence* for her incapacity. It also neglects the fact that *all* of us make choices by consulting our emotional and bodily responses, sometimes at a subconscious level.

And the opposite extreme should encourage caution with this cognitivist bias, as explored by Louis Charland in his provocatively titled paper, 'Is Mr. Spock mentally competent?' (1998). On paper, Mr. Spock is *the* ideal picture of rational decision-making capacity, setting aside emotion to use cool, clear logic in every circumstance. But in the 2009 version of *Star Trek*, the fact that Spock behaves in this detached, rational manner, especially after he witnesses the death of his mother and destruction of his planet, Vulcan, is *precisely* why James Kirk believes Spock lacks the ability to make decisions as acting captain. The absence of emotion can also be an indication that our decision-making capacity is compromised in some way – in short, Mr. Spock is not always mentally competent. Emotion and absorbed bodily coping provide important cues to our choices – they can make us agents who respond appropriately to a situation, they can alert us to relevant features in our environment – and how these emotional and bodily capacities translate to decision-making capacity may not be fully captured if we are not at least alive to the cognitive bias in the functional test.

The interactions of assessment

So far, much of this book has emphasised how conditions within a person's circle of support can affect her autonomy and in turn, her capacity to make decisions. This is why hermeneutic competence is vital within a person's circle of support. Equally, assessors need to acquire these skills in the *interactions of assessment* – how the assessment itself is carried out, the manner of communicating with the person with impairment. There are two parts to this: first, assessors should *meet* with the person who is being assessed; second, the interaction needs to be carried out using skills of hermeneutic competence, to ensure a participatory and enabling ethos prevails.

First, the very baseline for any assessment should be extended, first-hand dialogue and conversation with the person being assessed. This is not to deny the various practical challenges – it might mean a financial commitment, overcoming logistical challenges, the very real problem of extremely busy practitioners, often underpaid and underappreciated, sometimes lacking relevant training, spread too thinly over a heavy caseload. This means that it can sometimes be tempting to rely as much, if not more, on the observations of others, with only a limited 'snapshot' personal assessment.

But reliance on medical notes or professional testimony can only get us so far. Think of what happens in the course of written correspondence. For instance, a work colleague might have a habit of writing terse, short sentences in her correspondence. Just reading it I might think, 'how awfully rude', or 'she must be cross with me'. I add all my own interpretative baggage into how I understand the tone of the email. Or I might read the person who likes to use emoticons in his texts as 'immature' or 'overeffusive'. Misinterpreting written communication is all too easy. But on meeting the 'presumed rude-one-line' colleague or 'overeffusive user-of-emoticons', my preliminary conclusions might be overturned: the 'rude' colleague is warm and generous, while the emoticon user considerate with appropriate gravity.

The limitations of written communication are even more evident when it comes in the form of a psychiatrist's notes along the lines of 'Rachel suffers from *x* disorder and discussion with her indicates that she lacks insight into the nature of her illness.' Reading a sentence like that, we may be naturally more inclined to believe the psychiatrist (as the expert) and adopt the view that Rachel *must* lack capacity, even with our best intentions to think otherwise. But an assessor who actually talks with Rachel might come to a completely different conclusion to that of her psychiatrist, that she *does* understand the nature of her illness but deeply resents her institutionalisation and the sense of powerlessness over her care. What is 'lack of insight' to one is understandable frustration and even conscious rebellion to another. When we engage in a detailed dialogue with someone in person, we have an opportunity to get a better sense of her perspective, what she means and what motivates her.

Conversation and dialogue are also important because the fine line between paternalistic and autonomy-promoting interventions lies precisely in the interactions that occur between practitioners and the person. First-hand dialogue with individuals puts a 'face' to the decision that one makes as an assessor, placing at the forefront how it will impact on that person.

Importantly, this still leaves disagreement about what 'participation' means, particularly in the context of the MCA and CRPD. Some suggest that it means that the person is to have *input* into the decision; others say that such input is dependent on how close a person is on the border threshold of capacity; yet others claim that participation means the individual's decision is *determinative* – as in, practitioners need to respect and implement that decision. There is scope to have this argument, but that isn't our focus here. Regardless of how we define participation, it is still the case that it ought to be encouraged in principle, and the way to do it in the first instance is to meet and engage with the individual first-hand: to 'humanise' a process that can be intrusive and burdensome for those with impairments.

The second aspect of *interactions of assessment* is that we can meet with the person, but assessment could still be done poorly. Something else is needed if these are used as genuine opportunities to try and understand her standpoint and choices. Skills of hermeneutic competence, where the assessor is attuned to impairment, recognises the person, and engages in open dialogue with an overall stance of humility, will help ensure that the interactions of assessment accord with an ethos of enablement and participation. By way of illustration, consider the example of Paul who has a moderate learning disability and is being assessed as to whether he has capacity to remain within his mother's care and, if not, to determine what is in his best interests. Perhaps at the time he is adamant that he wants to stay with her, despite the fact that she hits him occasionally, regularly denigrates him and his abilities, and they both live in squalid, unhealthy conditions. Practitioners might have a good sense that any potential autonomy skills he might have are being suppressed by living with her. But this assessment could be carried out in two ways. A disabling assessment might have any or all of the following features:

- The assessor meets with Paul as a 'token', gesture, relying instead on case notes provided by the social worker and psychiatrist, and makes a decision based on these notes.

- The assessor asks leading questions and doesn't reflect on the prejudices that might influence the way she approaches her interaction with Paul (i.e., his diagnosis means he is unlikely to be able to decide; she sets the bar high for the type of knowledge that is needed to make a decision).

- The assessor uses words that Paul doesn't understand and fails to use pictures where these might be useful.

- The assessor uses language in her conversation with Paul or others in his social care team that expresses doubt that Paul is unlikely to ever regain capacity, even if he is to be moved from his mother's care. The language used is focused on Paul's limitations rather than his potential.

By contrast, the interactions of a more enabling assessment would look markedly different:

- The assessor makes a point to set aside sufficient time to meet with Paul, gain his trust and talk about what is important to him. She is attuned to the way that his body and emotions might interact and cope with his environment, and how these may reflect skilful ways of navigating his situation.

- The assessor is careful to reflect on the prejudices which inevitably frame her perspective and tries to be open to Paul's own way of interpreting himself and his circumstances. She doesn't adopt the view, 'Paul is the same as everyone else with this learning impairment', but rather, 'Paul is a person with his own unique take on things'.

- She asks open questions and uses whatever tools that are needed to communicate with Paul. When she has difficulty understanding Paul's response, she tries to repeat it in a different way using simple words and pictures.

- The assessor recognises that language matters: she is careful to ensure that she uses enabling language, focused on Paul's potential, abilities and future autonomy skills, to frame any decision that is being made.

Importantly, we are not saying interventions are illegitimate. Paul's situation may indeed warrant intervention, where his removal from his mother's care will promote the flourishing of his autonomy skills and decision-making capabilities. But the line between legitimate and illegitimate interventions often lies with *how* the interactions of assessment are carried out. For that, we need to be committed truly to meeting the individual in the first place, and then being attentive to whether we are using key hermeneutical skills to ensure our interactions are appropriately focused on enabling persons with impairment, thus mitigating the power inequality that is inimical to assessment.

Case study

In proceedings before the Court of Protection, a learning disability psychiatrist had provided a report to the court, concluding that a young man lacked capacity to make decisions as to his residence, care and contact arrangements with his family. An independent social worker was asked to consider the young man's best interests. In the course of the very detailed work to draw out his wishes and feelings, with the use of resources such as drawings to make concrete abstract concepts such as 'trust', the independent social worker was able to achieve such detailed responses that the judge in the case took the view that, in fact, the young man might have capacity. The judge therefore ordered a further assessment of the young man's capacity, and, ultimately, concluded that he *had capacity to make all the relevant decisions in his life*. The High Court made orders under the inherent jurisdiction regulating his contact with his father to secure him against the pressure being exerted on him by the father.

[See LBX v K & Ors [2013] EWHC 3230 (Fam) and [2013] EWHC 4170 (Fam).]

The reparative potential of assessment

Assessors are in a unique position to evaluate and recommend certain courses of action within a person's circle of support. One aspect that isn't mentioned much is how assessments can be the beginning of a process of *narrative repair* – narrative practices that help overturn damage to an individual's personal identity.

So far, we have discussed the dual function of practitioners in relation to a person's circle of support: they are *part* of that circle, but they can also take a *step backwards*, to adopt the more evaluative stance of an assessor, which helps identify situations and circumstances where narratives are destructive, abusive, discriminatory or disabling to the person with impairment. This evaluative role does imply power and its potential misuse. But equally, this role helps *call out* disabling, abusive narratives and practices – naming them as unacceptable and effectively *initiating* a process of narrative repair. Narrative repair uses counter-stories to help individuals resist disabling ways of understanding themselves (Lindemann Nelson 2001), to cultivate the nurturing relations-to-self we discussed in the previous chapter. These encourage individuals to see themselves as worthy of respect, trust and esteem, as persons with potential autonomy skills who deserve inclusion and consideration. The transient nature of their interactions might mean that assessors are unlikely to be part and parcel of this process, but they nonetheless 'set the tone' of future interpersonal interactions, acting as an important check – as a 'conscience' – to those within a person's circle of support. A shift in perspective from the very top of the chain (like a judge at the Court of Protection) can affect practices all the way down, from assessment to daily care, motivating strategies and narratives that establish a more empowering agenda which bolsters a person's participation, inclusion and decision-making abilities.

This may give the misleading impression that professionals can intervene regardless of a person's wishes. But in fact, decisions *not* to intervene are equally possible (see the case study below). The type of narrative repair that assessors can initiate comes in multiple forms of support – whether this be in the form of providing family support or reigning in the protective impulses of the local authority, or indeed, interventions to remove a person who is so evidently neglected and abused. Thinking about this process of narrative repair is important because it adds further tools to distinguish between those types of interventions that can be legitimate and enabling and those that are on shaky grounds and end up disrespecting the individual.

Case study

Janet, a woman with a moderate learning impairment, wants to live with her long-term partner, yet the professionals supporting her strongly oppose the relationship on grounds the she appears neglected and mistreated (e.g., she ends up dirty after their meetings or lost in town; he has spoken disdainfully to her in front of others). As a result, her care team restrict all contact with her partner, not allowing her any private meetings or phone calls with him. Janet strongly objects, claiming she loves her partner and has tried repeatedly to run away from residential care. Despite the views of the professionals, a third-party assessor might conclude it is *their* overprotectiveness that is disproportionate and damaging, effectively communicating to Janet that she is incapable of making decisions. On closer examination, the impulse to safeguard and protect is in fact *disabling* her autonomy skills and discouraging nurturing relations-to-self. This assessor starts to initiate the process of narrative repair by recommending that her care team respects Janet's privacy, and suggests that provisions ought to be made for her to meet privately with her partner; she speaks of Janet in a manner which emphasises supporting and enabling her decision-making abilities rather than protecting her.

[Inspired by the decision in Re MM (an adult) [2007] EWHC 2003 (Fam).]

Summary

Assessments can be intrusive and burdensome for persons with impairments. We have suggested that capacity and best interests assessors have an ethical role, partly due to the very simple reason that assessment in and of itself is a kind of intervention into a person's life. These interventions might start off as relatively minor – as when capacity is assessed through an informal conversation – but could lead to momentous implications for an individual – as when a person is removed from her home, prevented from marrying, or allowed to refuse treatment. Reflecting on one's ethical role means we can be encouraged to critically examine the assumptions we might import into our assessments, as well as prioritise truly *meeting* the individual – having a meaningful conversation and dialogue with her – so that interactions are fundamentally based on an ethos of enablement and participation, rather than disablement and exclusion.

Checklist of reflective questions

- What deeper principles or values (personal, professional, societal) orient my approach to capacity and best interests assessment?

- What is my attitude towards risk?

- What am I seeking to do when I assess someone's capacity?

- What am I seeking to do when I am involved in making a decision about what is in a person's best interests?

- If the language and reasoning that I use in relation to the individuals I am asked to assess was used in relation to me, would I think I was being enabled or empowered?

Chapter 6

Capacity and Best Interests

A Not-So-Bright Line

Two competing impulses

Thus far in the book we have discussed the importance of relationships in promoting the autonomy and decision-making abilities of individuals with impairments. In contexts of relational abuse, neglect and coercion, practitioners may feel pulled in two directions. From one direction there is a sense of duty to safeguard individuals from disabling relational environments: quite understandably, we don't want to leave individuals to live in squalid, unhealthy conditions, or to be subject to physical or emotional abuse at the hands of those around them. Practitioners often feel the impulse to intervene, to remove the person from these situations. From another direction, there is a sense of obligation to respect individuals and guard against unwarranted paternalism: the value of personal autonomy has become so central to, not just our daily lives, but also clinical treatment and social care. This impulse seems to recommend practitioners step aside, allowing individuals to get on with their own lives as they see fit. How do we reconcile these two seemingly irreconcilable impulses?

In fact, sometimes these two impulses simply cannot be resolved. Sometimes, it may be all but inevitable that the person's choice will mean the difference between life and death. In such a situation, to make a judgement between them is to assess the incomparable – values that are beyond comparison, beyond any common measure. And to actually make such a decision may mean our judgements appeal to those values that seem to be stronger, more convincing, more important – not necessarily to us personally, but to the collective values and convictions of our society (Hedley 2016).

But even as certain values are incomparable, one's judgements should not be arbitrary and lacking in critical reflection. In this book, we have already discussed certain considerations that practitioners need to include in their reflective arsenal if they hope to address or resolve such competing impulses in an effective and ethical manner:

- There is a need to adopt a more holistic, relational account of autonomy – one that starts from the view that individuals throughout their lives will require the support of others to facilitate their agency and autonomy skills (see Chapter 2).

- The skills of a hermeneutic competence – involving attunement to impairment, recognition of the person, and open dialogue and humility – are needed by those within a person's circle of support if they are to encourage these autonomy skills (see Chapter 3).

- Practitioners must be critically aware of when a person's decisions and sense of herself reflect incapacitating narratives (see Chapter 4).

- Equally, assessors require skills of hermeneutic competence if assessments are to accord with an ethos of enablement, regardless of whether a person has capacity or not. Any proposed interventions should be deeply sensitive to the context (see Chapter 5).

- Practitioners should acknowledge and engage with the ethical role they have as an assessor, mindful of their own value frameworks and prejudgements, and the interventionist nature of assessment in and of itself (see Chapter 5).

The last consideration we want to include in this list is the focus of this final chapter, namely:

- Practitioners should understand capacity and best interests as a *spectrum* rather than divided by a clear-cut boundary.

The prevailing view that a bright line separates capacity and best interests is oversimplistic: not only does it fail to track real-life practice among professionals, but it also limits the scope of obligations practitioners may have in many borderline and even clear-cut cases. Below we explore this in more detail.

Problems with capacity as a cliff-edge

The way that the MCA is currently set up gives the impression that a stark boundary exists between capacity and best interests. With the status of decision-making capacity, one can go ahead and make one's own choices; otherwise, what others think is within one's welfare can be imposed against one's wishes. Or as one of us has put it (Ruck Keene 2015a), this presents 'capacity as a cliff-edge off which one falls into the clinging embrace of paternalism'.

Clearly demarcated categories of 'capacity' and 'best interests' might seem useful, but they can form a blunt instrument. Commonly noted is how such a cliff-edge view could sanction the complete dismissal of the perspectives and values of the person at the heart of the decision if one is found on the 'wrong' side of the boundary (i.e., lacking capacity and subject to best interests decisions). Individuals don't just fall into the embrace of paternalism, but worse, their incapacity can be used as justification to disregard their views and preferences altogether. The further away they are from the cliff-edge, the less their views are taken into consideration, or the less they participate and are involved in the decisions that affect their lives.

We often worry about the cliff-edge towards paternalism, yet this cliff-edge can go the opposite way, where a finding of capacity means individuals *literally* falling – falling without support, suffering neglect, exploitation and/or abuse, without the assistance of others to help cushion the blow (or, indeed, avoid the blow altogether). The domestic abuse example from Chapter 2 is helpful here. Women who want to leave abusive partners are often unable to precisely because of the vacuum of support: the shortage of safe houses, the lack of law enforcement to investigate and prosecute abusers, the absence of financial assistance and so on. These all mean that should a woman leave her abusive situation, she literally has to make it on her own with no support mechanisms in place (keeping in mind that the pattern of abuse means she is already likely highly isolated, with few or no financial resources of her own). By comparison, consider the example of a young woman with a learning disability who is found to have capacity to consent to having sexual relations in circumstances where practitioners observe the men in her housing unit repeatedly exploiting her vulnerability, perhaps implicitly 'grooming' her for something illegal down the road. Does a finding of capacity mean that practitioners simply allow her to be sexually exploited by the men around her, where they do nothing, even if she says she 'likes' the attention? We *should* feel uncomfortable with this prospect, especially if a finding of decision-making capacity effectively means she is allowed to fall off the cliff-edge (e.g., perhaps become a victim of forced prostitution in the future) without any support to the contrary.

Ambiguities in the legal landscape

At a superficial level, the MCA's threshold concept of capacity does purportedly separate the right of autonomy and paternalistic welfare. Despite how clear-cut the boundary seems in the MCA, problems with a cliff-edge view of capacity have already been observed, making the legal landscape more complex than it initially appears. A finding of incapacity doesn't necessarily mean that paternalistic actions are appropriate, with legal judgments increasingly acknowledging the importance of the person's participation, voice and, indeed, autonomy, *even* in best interests decisions. Conversely, and as outlined in Chapter 1, the continued existence of the High Court's inherent jurisdiction further complicates this picture, where protective interventions can be sanctioned to safeguard capacitous but vulnerable individuals from harmful, malignant relationships and care environments. This suggests that certain protective duties and obligations to safeguard and promote a person's agency continue to exist even if individuals pass a legal threshold for decision-making capacity. And at the level of international human rights, the CRPD does away altogether with the categories of mental capacity and best interests. Instead, the concept of universal legal capacity recognises a spectrum of experiences and abilities among individuals with impairments which entitles them to a range of positive supports, protections and entitlements.

This is not to say that these different areas of the law coexist easily: most notably, debates around Article 12 of the CRPD question whether *any* judgments taken on a 'best interests' basis should be allowed, and whether the concept of mental capacity is fundamentally discriminatory. These are valid concerns, though we cannot explore them in this book, and it is likely that in due course the statutory landscape may well end up looking rather different from the way it does at present.

We ultimately believe that some statutory reform is necessary. But pending such reform, perhaps we can use the current complexities in the legal landscape to our advantage. The central focus of our book has been on the complex practices, relationships and contexts where capacity and best interests become an issue. Attempts to oversimplify these complexities mean we risk ignoring various important factors, whether this be how a person interacts and copes with her environment, or what skills and abilities are within her potential, or how those within her circle of support project certain enabling or disabling narratives, or how practitioners themselves can be encouraging or harmful influences in the process of assessment and intervention. The law is dealing with complex, multifaceted individuals embedded within supportive, relational circumstances which demand sensitivity and understanding. Whether or not we have impairments, all of us are an amalgam of strengths and weaknesses, capabilities and lack of ability. Within the same person might be the ability to write or practise law and the inability to do maths, or the capacity for great logical thinking but the absence of emotional intelligence. Within the same relationship can be genuine love and caring but also a tendency to smother and protect or neglect and disregard. The function of the law is to be properly responsive to such complexities, without which it functions as a blunt instrument, blind to individuals and their circumstances. Some might qualify as clear-cut cases of incapacity (e.g., someone in a permanently vegetative state) but many (if not most) reside in the blurry boundary between capacity and best interests.

Thus, practitioners might reach black and white judgements about capacity and best interests, but this is within an ambiguous legal landscape that we can – potentially – mould to the unique circumstances of individuals and complex relational dynamics. From the direction of capacity, *even if* a person has capacity, practitioners may still have an obligation to intervene in harmful circumstances (as we see with the continued use of the inherent jurisdiction). From the direction of best interests, *even if* a person lacks capacity, practitioners may have a duty to facilitate the person's participation and involvement in the best interests decision (as evident in the MCA's participatory ethos, and even more strongly put in the CRPD, where the person with impairment lies at the heart of every decision). Whichever direction one starts from in the law, the implication is that capacity and best interests form part of a *spectrum* rather than occupy opposite sides of a cliff.

A spectrum view

One reason why the cliff-edge view of capacity remains so deeply entrenched is because our notions of impairment and disability tend to adhere to either-or categories: one is 'impaired' or not, one has a 'disability' or is so-called 'able-bodied' (both of which are concepts criticised for their derogatory connotations). Even with a greater understanding of impairments, our frame of reference still veers towards these out-dated binary concepts. But compare this with the examples above of the person who can write well but is utterly hopeless at sums, or who is intellectually clever but emotionally challenged: we are unlikely to reduce either person to his faulty maths ability or her limited emotional range. When we try and get a sense of what a person is about, we are inclined to think of her holistically – of the interplay of her different skills, or how these skills manifest themselves in other contexts. The question then is, why is there an overwhelming tendency to focus purely on 'the impairment' of the individual, for instance to assess whether or not *this quality in particular* (or, indeed, *its absence*) impacts on her decision-making capacity? Rather than taking abilities and weaknesses as facets of a whole person which manifest themselves differently depending on context, we just focus on the traits that are perceived to be 'lacking'.

But a spectrum approach to capacity and best interests pushes against this tendency and starts from the premise that *there is a multidimensional range of subjective abilities, experiences and meaningful relationships*. Classifications of disability are in fact moving away from discrete, binary categorisations towards a more multifaceted view which treats functioning and disability as universal phenomena that everyone experiences over their lifetime. The World Health Organization's International Classification of Functioning, Disability and Health (ICF) places health and disability on a multidimensional spectrum based on the interplay between the person and environment (at the levels of the body, person and society) (WHO 2002) (see Figure 6.1).

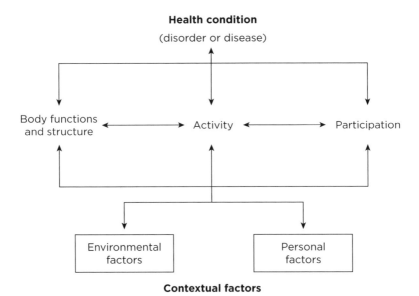

Figure 6.1: Model of disability for ICF (source: WHO 2002)

Based on the ICF, an intellectual disability like Down syndrome (Figure 6.2) is a multidimensional, integrated phenomenon that includes participation restrictions, environmental barriers as well as individual impairments and limitations involving body functions, personal factors and activity skills (Arvidsson *et al.* 2008). The interplay between contextual, environmental/personal factors and individual functioning is accounted for, meaning that difficulties in participation or activity skills can coexist with capacities and abilities in different environments. Moreover, restrictions and skills will involve evaluations by observers *as well as self-rated, first-personal accounts.*

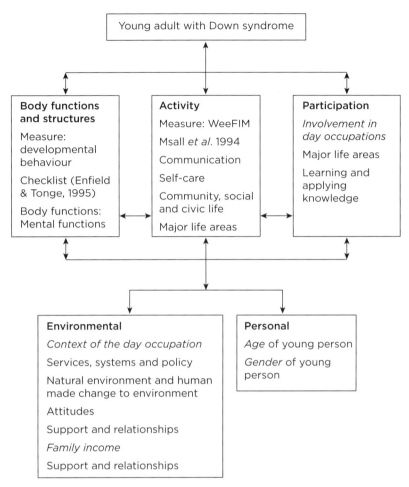

Figure 6.2: Example of young adult with Down syndrome using the ICF (source: Foley *et al.* 2014)

The ICF highlights how adherence to a binary picture of capacity and incapacity appears outdated and simplistic. The conceptual understanding of disability is changing to reflect a more holistic, multidimensional and contextual model of capacities and limitations, one which moves beyond a narrow lens on the diagnosis and functioning levels of the individual, to one that explores how environmental factors can also impact on a person's ability to participate and share in different activities (Foley *et al.* 2014).

This more holistic picture of disability lends itself naturally to a spectrum approach to capacity and best interests. Using a scalar rather than binary lens, individuals and their range of abilities are assessed taking into consideration how these interact with environmental factors. Between respect for autonomy and safeguarding lies a wide range of options: safeguarding decisions might aim to protect emotional well-being and physical health, or they could also be focused on protecting a person's agency and the conditions that enable her ability to decide (Figure 6.3).

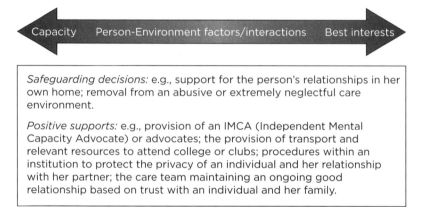

Capacity   Person-Environment factors/interactions   Best interests

Safeguarding decisions: e.g., support for the person's relationships in her own home; removal from an abusive or extremely neglectful care environment.

Positive supports: e.g., provision of an IMCA (Independent Mental Capacity Advocate) or advocates; the provision of transport and relevant resources to attend college or clubs; procedures within an institution to protect the privacy of an individual and her relationship with her partner; the care team maintaining an ongoing good relationship based on trust with an individual and her family.

Figure 6.3: A spectrum view

Some blurring between best interests judgements and capacity assessments therefore seems inevitable. Wriggle room both ways is already implied in the case law, with some judgments indicating that one's distance to the threshold of capacity will determine the extent of one's participation or how seriously one's views and values are considered.[1]

From the angle of best interests, capacity considerations bleeding into best interests judgements might be good thing: the enabling, empowering agenda around a person does not stop, nor should it, just because someone might lack capacity. The participation of the person, her perspective and values, should be just as important as

---

1   See, for instance, *Re ITW* [2009] EWHC 2525 (Fam).

if she was found to have capacity. As Peter Jackson J states in *Wye Valley NHS Trust v Mr B* [2015] EWCOP 60:

> As the Act [MCA] and the European Convention make clear, a conclusion that a person lacks decision-making capacity is not an '*off-switch*' for his rights and freedoms. To state the obvious, the wishes and feelings, beliefs and values of people with a mental disability are as important to them as they are to anyone else, and may even be more important. It would therefore be wrong in principle to apply any automatic discount to their point of view. (para. 11)

From the opposite angle, however, the blurring of best interests considerations into capacity adjudications seems less desirable. This would seem to leave the door open to capacity assessments that import questionable values or make illegitimate judgements about a person's decisions, thus fundamentally disrespecting the individual being assessed. Would a spectrum view make this even worse, violating the core value of personal autonomy that the concept of capacity is designed to protect?

There are two responses to this. Our first point speaks to the worry that a spectrum view imports the types of judgements that are more characteristic of best interests decisions, such as considerations about welfare or the person's good. In principle, these put capacity assessments on tenuous ground. But assessors have to deliberate from *somewhere*, and sometimes, it might be the case that one's starting point *is* some kind of value judgement. This is not necessarily a problem. Where it *does* become problematic is when these values and assumptions are implicit and unacknowledged, and important aspects of our deliberation remain hidden. Such tendencies become more pronounced the more we hold fast to the mistaken vision of the assessor as a neutral observer. Capacity assessments inevitably import assumptions and judgements of some kind – we went through a range of these in the previous chapter. But good practices of assessment encourage critical reflection and self-awareness, in order to:

- view these values and assumptions as *provisional* and subject to change

- develop an orientation of genuine openness and comportment of respect towards the person at the centre of assessment

- subject these values to proper critical debate and public discussion, so that practices around assessment can be evaluated according to an ethos of enablement and empowerment.

For example, consider the continued use of the court's inherent jurisdiction. One might dismiss this as a legal fudge to extend the paternalistic protection of individuals, particularly where the MCA doesn't provide the outcome we want (i.e., a person has capacity and therefore we cannot subject her to a best interests decision). Yet the use of inherent jurisdiction also speaks to an essentially intuitive (but as we have spelled out above, justified) view that relational circumstances of coercion, exploitation and so on are problematic and can can impede a person's abilities of self-care and of making authentic choices that are independent of the pressure or threats of others. It also speaks of an intuition to defend and protect the interests of those who are more vulnerable – if due to some physical frailty or cognitive limitation, they are susceptible to violations of their property, bodily integrity or agency. If practitioners fail to explore the underlying values, presumptions and reasons for the use of the inherent jurisdiction, we have no critical resources to openly question, clarify or change the types of reasons we *do* think are valid as opposed to those that aren't.

This leads to our second point. The worry about best interests considerations seeping into capacity assessment depends on a particular understanding of autonomy. If we believe autonomy functions *only* as a shield which guards us against outside intervention – that is, its core is the right to be left alone – this worry makes sense. But Chapter 2 already outlined reasons why the shield concept of autonomy is too limited. A firm demarcation between capacity and best interests tends to hive off obligations to promote autonomy – to provide the positive supports that are so crucial to enabling the decision-making abilities and agency of those with impairments. By contrast, a spectrum view is better aligned with a more nuanced understanding of autonomy and the complexities it involves. Not only can we *respect* autonomy, it can also be *promoted, encouraged, fostered* and *facilitated* – actions which require the assistance of others as well as structural provisions in the legal, political and social sphere. As articulated so powerfully in the CRPD, positive supports are necessary if persons with impairment are to be treated as equal participants in society, and these are owed to individuals *whether or not they are found to have capacity*. Realising those positive supports is not always easy, especially where it requires the expenditure of public money;[2] we can at least strive to achieve the best that we can within the constraints that are imposed on us, while seeking to challenge those constraints.

Summary

On a spectrum view, mental capacity isn't an arbitrary cut-off point that determines whether individuals are supported or not. This isn't to say that all assistance – even unwanted – should be forced on the unwilling individual. But equally, the scope for providing interventions and assistance to those who might, on a very narrow view, have capacity needs to be more elastic to accommodate the complexity that so often characterises the rich lives of individuals who require varying levels of support and care.

---

2   The Supreme Court has made clear, for instance, that decisions made as to what is in a person's best interests have to be made as a choice between options that are actually available: *N v ACGG* [2017] UKSC 22.

Chapter 7

Conclusion

In this book, we have mainly focused on complexities that practitioners encounter and we have provided different considerations that should be taken into account in dealing with these. Complexities shouldn't be shied away from, nor should they be approached with a one-size-fits-all solution. To adopt such an approach would ignore how those with impairments are *persons* – they are individuals with unique personalities, multifaceted abilities and potential, who, like the rest of us, can flourish given the right circumstances. We have tried to show that tendencies towards an overly individualistic, cognitivist and simplistic approach to questions about capacity, autonomy and decision-making do a disservice to persons with impairments and also ignore the complex web of relational, social and structural supports that is needed to enable their equal participation and recognition.

Practitioners must acknowledge their own roles in enhancing the autonomy of individuals, to ensure that their engagement is based on an ethos of enablement and inclusion. And in order to do this, we need to focus on what skills and capacities are needed on *our behalf.* So often the focus is on the other person – what *she* needs, what *she* purportedly lacks. But practitioners and assessors have a great responsibility to understand, interpret and enable individuals whose views and abilities are all too often ignored or devalued in our society. Honest discussion and critical reflection will be vital, alongside an orientation of genuine openness and humility towards others and their different ways of expressing what matters to them.

To summarise: what does this all mean for practice and how practitioners should go about assessment?

1. A key purpose of this book has been to equip practitioners with a set of *ethical* justifications which would enable them to take a more expansive – relational – view of mental capacity. Especially in the context of those who are in social situations that are disabling their autonomy, we are – therefore – arguing that practitioners should be readier to conclude that the individual lacks capacity to make key decisions such as whether to continue to live in that situation. However, and so as to comply with the law as it stands, it will always be necessary to spell out how the individual's inability to make that decision is caused by an identified disturbance or impairment in the functioning of her mind or brain. We suggest that it is often going to be most useful to examine whether the individual's impairment prevents her from being able to understand, use or weigh the information that others around her may have interests contrary to hers.

2. Crucially, if a capacity assessor has proceeded as above and concluded that the individual *does* lack capacity to take the relevant decision, then the onus is on the assessor and those around him to secure the provision of the necessary supports for the individual to enable her to (re)gain capacity.

3. Even under the framework set out above, there will still be cases where it is simply not possible to say that the individual lacks the relevant decision-making capacity. At that point, and if the situation of the individual causes sufficient concern, it is very likely that recourse will be required to the inherent jurisdiction, unless it is possible to invoke domestic violence legislation (such as a Domestic Violence Protection Notice or the potential criminal offence of coercive and controlling behaviour in an intimate or familial relationship under s.76 of the Serious Crimes Act 2015).

4. Any relief that is asked for under the inherent jurisdiction should be directed, so far as possible, against those who may be exercising coercion and control over the individual. It can only ever be legitimate to direct relief against the individual concerned when all else has failed. If the situation will amount to a deprivation of liberty (i.e., she will be confined at, say, the respite placement, and does not consent to that confinement), then it can only be justified where the individual is of 'unsound mind' and it is necessary and proportionate to the risk to which she would be exposed otherwise). Any relief directed against the individual must always have in mind the central purpose of fostering her health, welfare, dignity and self-respect.

5. In cases where the individual is not subject to coercion or control at the hands of another, there is very much less scope for taking the expansive approach to the causative nexus we have set out. There may still be circumstances where the individual is not able to make decisions as to matters such as where she should live as a result of the combination of her mental impairment and the effects of the environment around her. And there may well also be cases where the individual is not able to understand, retain, use or weigh information about the harmful effect of living in such an environment on her. But in general, in such cases, we must look much more closely at whether we can assist the individual to make her own decisions through the conventional tools of support. There is, we suggest, considerably less room to justify seeking to conclude that the individual lacks capacity in the relevant domain so as to be able to take empowering steps in her best interests.

6. Crucially, we should emphasise that adopting the 'spectrum' approach we have outlined above may, in many cases, lead assessors ultimately to take steps that might, instinctively, have felt very uncomfortable, whether that be supporting an

individual in a decision to refuse medical treatment which could – it appears – save her life, or embarking on a course of action which appears to be profoundly risky. However, a key purpose of the ethical tools that we have set out in the body of this book is to help assessors test, check and refine their instincts: at a minimum, therefore, assessors should be able to give a convincing answer as to *why* they have taken the steps that they have taken regarding any individual with impairments.

Appendices

Theoretical Resources

Much of the academic research in this book comes from Camillia Kong, *Mental Capacity in Relationship: Decision-Making, Dialogue, and Autonomy* (Cambridge University Press, 2017). Reference to that book is worthwhile for a much deeper philosophical and legal discussion of many of the issues discussed here. These appendices provide a basic overview of some of the theoretical background behind various concepts and arguments within this book, as well as some further reading which practitioners may find useful. We are aware that issues in the book are the subject of literature from a social work lens, but the justifactory basis for this book ultimately comes from a philosophical perspective.

Appendix 1: Autonomy

The concept of autonomy is philosophically complicated and nuanced. In Western liberal society, autonomy denotes the ability to govern oneself and one's life without any alien or external influences. Or in other words, autonomy is a feature of the will that enables us to make authentic and consistent choices for ourselves. Autonomy so understood often focuses on the individual, where *respecting* personal autonomy means we defer to one's subjective choices.

What we might call the 'standard model' of autonomy asserts that certain conditions are necessary for autonomy, including consistency and authenticity. *Consistency* refers to the competencies and skills that help us make psychologically coherent choices: the ability to deliberate, reason and exercise self-control in making choices that comply with our values, such that we can endorse such choices on critical reflection. For example, a person who gives to charity in line with her long-standing value about the importance of giving to those less fortunate is making a psychologically consistent choice. This psychological consistency helps fulfil the condition of *authenticity*: our choices reflect the *authentic self* so that when this person gives to charity, she is revealing and acting in a way that expresses her true self and her true values.

But the conditions of autonomy are far more complex than this standard picture suggests. This complexity matters when we start to consider:

- cases where psychopathology and disorder are egosyntonic (i.e., consistent with personal identity and values; eating and personality disorders are often seen to be egosytonic, and individuals can speak of their autism, bipolar disorder and schizophrenia as an important part of who they are)

- cases where relational abuse and societal/structural oppression affect the shaping of personal identity and values

(i.e., when harmful values around gender and race are internalised and replicated)

- cases where individuals and their agency require a network of support and interdependency (i.e., when the decision-making of persons with impairments is interactive with those around them, where advice from their circle of support is needed to make a decision).

These can be problematic cases to make sense of according to the standard account of autonomy: cases of egosyntonic disorder would appear to fulfil conditions of psychological consistency and authenticity, while the presence or absence of relational support is a side issue that seems to be irrelevant to autonomy. The standard model fails to identify what has gone awry in the *formation* of decision-making skills in egosyntonic disorders, and views as heteronomous those individuals who require the help of others to exercise autonomy skills. This indicates two weaknesses with the standard model: (1) it is too individualistic, focusing narrowly on the internal aspects of decision-making to the neglect of the social and relational dimensions that help develop our personal identity and enable us to exercise decision-making capacities; (2) it is too cognitive, focusing on the intellectual skills of critical thinking and reasoning to the neglect of the emotional and perceptual skills that enable us to cope skilfully with our environment.

Relational accounts of autonomy try to address such weaknesses. Relational autonomy emerged largely out of feminist concerns around the inability of the 'standard account' of autonomy to capture the experiences of women in two respects: first, the impact of oppressive socialisation on women's agency and autonomy; second, the dismissal of interdependency and relationality in its idealisation of typically male agency, characterised by self-sufficiency and rugged independence. Feminist critiques outline a more nuanced picture of autonomy, which seeks to consider the *relational and social circumstances that help shape a person's identity and practical agency.* Self-determination is developed through socially acquired 'autonomy competencies': a range of perceptual, emotional as well as cognitive skills needed to make consistent choices and foster authentic selves (Meyers 1989). Relational autonomy not only helps embed personal autonomy within relational and social support, but provides crucial theoretical resources to help identify instances where social conditioning has been harmful for personal autonomy. Coercion, oppression, abuse, neglect and structural inequality become core rather than side issues for autonomy, so that we consider, not just how individuals make choices (i.e., the actual decision-making procedure) but also the dynamic process of how an authentic self develops through the continual interplay of individual characteristics and the conditions within one's social and relational context.

As a result, the assessment of the capacities that personal autonomy requires becomes a spectrum rather than an either-or scenario: we can have certain autonomy skills but lack others, and varying degrees of compartmentalisation will mean we exercise more or less autonomy in certain spheres of our lives. Equally, autonomy skills will involve not just cognitive capacities, but the everyday bodily, perceptual and emotional coping skills of individuals. Someone with an intellectual impairment might not be able to think and plan for her life ten years down the road, but her particular acts of everyday coping could still express 'pockets' of autonomy.

In summary, the standard model struggles to accommodate the experiences of 'limiting' or 'contrast' cases – those with cognitive impairments or mental disorder, those who experience oppressive socialising conditions or require substantial support to express themselves and act in the world. The conditions of relational autonomy, by contrast, are not so stringent as to automatically exclude individuals with impairments, but remain alive to the reality that all human beings require a web of relationship, support and interdependence in order to make choices that express authentic and self-determining selves.

Further recommended reading

Benson, Paul. (1994). 'Free agency and self-worth.' *Journal of Philosophy* 91: 650–668.

Dreyfus, Hubert L. (2014). *Skillful Coping: Essays on the Phenomenology of Everyday Perception and Action.* Oxford: Oxford University Press.

Dworkin, Gerald. (1976). 'Autonomy and behavior control.' *Hastings Center Report* 6: 23–28.

Frankfurt, Harry. (1971). 'Freedom of the will and the concept of a person.' *Journal of Philosophy* 68: 5–20.

Mackenzie, Catriona and Stoljar, Natalie (eds.). (2000). *Relational Autonomy: Feminist Perspectives on Autonomy, Agency, and the Social Self.* New York, NY: Oxford University Press.

Meyers, Diana T. (1989). *Self, Society, and Personal Choice.* New York, NY: Columbia University Press.

Appendix 2: The concept of disability

Our concept of disability has undergone substantial changes since the time when it was socially acceptable to refer to individuals with impairment as 'handicapped' or 'disfigured'. The language of disability is deeply powerful, and activists have rightly challenged the problematic assumptions contained within concepts such as 'normal function' or 'able-bodied'. Yet, the theoretical terrain around disability is deeply contested.

The medical model of disability might be largely discredited among disability rights advocates, service users and legal practitioners, but it remains firmly entrenched (albeit implicitly) within many clinical settings and, indeed, can be detected within a narrow interpretation of the causative nexus approach to mental capacity. The medical model attributes disability to intrinsic or biological causes, with an emphasis on managing and/or intervening to treat the purported defects within an individual's bodily functioning. Critics accuse the medical model of promoting an intrinsically disrespectful orientation towards individuals with impairments, where they are not treated as *persons* but reduced to socially undesirable features of their bodies. The intent is to 'fix' individuals and their impairments, rather than change the structural, relational and environmental barriers that systematically deprive persons with impairment of equal treatment and participation in society, whether through coercive paternalistic treatments or the absence of necessary economic and social entitlements.

Philosophical theories of personhood likewise struggle to understand and accommodate the experience of disability. This might seem a sidelong debate, but it is important. For example, the notion of human rights is grounded in the idea of the inherent dignity of persons, where the status of 'personhood' confers due respect and consideration by others. Disability challenges the standard ideal of personhood, raising important questions about the criteria that should distinguish between 'persons' and 'non-persons' – is this boundary based on the ability to think, cognise, reason? Or the potential to act on moral principles? Or human species membership? Or the capacity to feel pain and pleasure and hold certain interests as important? A threshold set 'too low' would raise difficult questions around whether animals and even plants qualify as persons who warrant equal treatment to humans beings; set 'too high', we risk relegating a range of human beings to the status of 'non-persons' who may not be entitled to equal respect and consideration. Indeed, a tendency to theorise about 'ideal' conditions means philosophical approaches to personhood can likewise struggle to understand and properly conceptualise the experience of disability and what is morally owed to persons with impairments.

Perhaps the most influential account of disability is the *social model*, developed by Michael Oliver in the 1970s (2009). The social model makes an important distinction between *impairment* and *disability*: impairment represents certain features of the body and its functioning, but disability is socially constructed, resulting from unequal structural features within society. In other words, impairment in and of itself is value neutral – meaning that it is neither 'good' nor 'bad'. These features of the body become 'good' or 'bad' because of the social meanings which become attached to these bodily features, as expressed in societal structures and barriers. For example, there is nothing inherently wrong with a paraplegic whose impairment demands the use of a wheelchair; where it becomes a disability is when society fails to accommodate his wheelchair use – like the absence of ramps – effectively excluding him from participating equally in social life and treating him like a second-class citizen.

As discussed throughout this book, the social model has become profoundly important – evident not least in the fact that the United Nations Convention on the Rights of Persons with Disabilities expressly adopts the social model as the justificatory framework for the rights and obligations that are owed to those with impairments. Emphasis is on the *accommodation* and *acceptance* of bodily difference in all its forms, positive duties and supports, and changing *societal, political and environmental structures* to promote the equal participation and respect of people with impairments. This has also led to a radical re-orientation in mental health and capacity law, where the permissibility of substituted decision-making mechanisms has become openly questioned. The logic is that treating individuals with impairments *differently* means they are treated *unequally*, and indeed, it is the right of *all* individuals to have the dignity of risk in making choices about their lives.

The social model provides an important lens for political advocacy efforts to improve the recognition and participation of persons with impairments. However, the social model is limited theoretically. According to what we might call an *interactionist account of disability*, the social model mistakenly downplays the inconveniences and residual difficulties caused by bodily impairment (see Shakespeare 2006). On this account, disability isn't just socially constructed, but involves the interaction between individual bodily factors and social barriers. Even after social barriers are removed, disabling features may continue to exist, due to the nature of a person's bodily impairment. Disability therefore involves the interplay between both intrinsic and extrinsic factors, and disregarding residual predicaments of an individual's bodily impairment could mean that we also fail to treat that person equally in a substantive sense. For example, the atrophy of muscles and the resulting pain and discomfort are intrinsic features of bodily impairment in Rett syndrome, while extrinsic factors, like water and physical therapy, might try to alleviate this. The resultant disability will be the interplay between bodily impairment and the efforts (or lack thereof) by the surrounding community and society. But even with the active and inclusive supports of those around her, the girl with Rett Syndrome might still struggle with muscular pain.

How we perceive disability has significant implications because it will justify the obligations and duties that we think are owed to those with impairments. Should these obligations and duties focus entirely on changing society and the community? Should these be based on respecting individuals and their choices in their private life, effectively treating those with and without impairments exactly the same? Or do our obligations demand an acknowledgement of bodily difference, its residual difficulties and efforts to alleviate these vulnerabilities, even if individuals don't necessarily want this assistance? These are difficult questions to answer. The medical and social models in isolation capture only a partial picture of disability, and likewise, philosophical accounts of personhood can be too restrictive, meaning that each provides an incomplete account of what obligations are owed to those with impairments. For these reasons we ultimately favour the interactionist picture of disability as providing the most holistic picture of disability and the complexities involved in relational, environmental and social support.

Further recommended reading

Kittay, Eva Feder. (2005). 'At the margins of personhood.' *Ethics* 116: 100–131.

McMahan, Jeff. (2003). *The Ethics of Killing: Problems at the Margins of Life.* New York, NY: Oxford University Press.

Oliver, Michael. (2009). *Understanding Disability: From Theory to Practice* (second edition). Basingstoke; New York, NY: Palgrave Macmillan.

Shakespeare, Tom. (2006). *Disability Rights and Wrongs.* London: Routledge.

United Nations Committee on the Rights of Persons with Disabilities. (April 2014). *General Comment No. 1 – Article 12: Equal Recognition Before the Law.* UN Doc. No. CRPD/C/GC/1, adopted at the 11th Session.

Appendix 3: Gadamer and hermeneutics

The discussion of hermeneutic competence in Chapter 3 draws mainly from Hans-Georg Gadamer's account of hermeneutics in *Truth and Method* (2004), where he explores the interpretive orientation and practices that are needed to understand human actions, texts and words in a meaningful manner. What is unique about Gadamer's approach is his critique of the 'prejudice against prejudice' (where there is a negative prejudice against the very concept of prejudice). In the philosophical and colloquial sense of the word, prejudices often have a negative connotation – they are seen as false, blinding, unfounded judgements. They aren't productive sources of knowledge; indeed, to gain knowledge we have to remain 'neutral' or 'objective' in our thinking. In contrast, Gadamer reclaims the 'positive' function of prejudice, as literally a *prejudgement*: a provisional judgement, verdict or decision that is valid prior to a final judgement. In this sense, prejudice makes it possible for us to understand and interpret in the first place; it forms a 'horizon' that effectively structures what we see and what is possible from our perspective. Prejudice will always shape the way in which we come to interpret and understand meaningful human action and communication. The fact that our horizon is formed of a range of prejudices reveals the *socially embedded* and *historical* nature of our perspective and conceptual schemes: our beliefs, our way of thinking, are embedded within linguistic, social, cultural and intellectual traditions which help frame our vision of and engagement with the world.

This seems a fairly obvious point – we all start from views and opinions which we absorb from our social, cultural and historical context. But crucially, Gadamer does not think that knowledge and interpretive understanding depends on us *transcending* this context. As mentioned, we often think that we need to distance ourselves from our prejudices in order to understand, interpret 'correctly', and gain knowledge, where we *disengage* from the social meanings which embed our own viewpoint. This picture of disengagement and impartial knowledge holds considerable sway in Western philosophy, particularly since Descartes. But Gadamer fundamentally resists this vision of the disengaged, idealised knower on two grounds: first, technical mastery over prejudice (by deploying some 'objective' method of interpretation) is impossible, even if we strive to become fully conscious of its influence. Second, as soon as we adopt this disengaging move, we don't actually rid ourselves of our prejudices – instead, we become even more blinded in assuming that they don't exist, making us even less likely to subject them to critical reflection. Prejudice is in fact an important part of developing and maturing our viewpoints, similar to the way our horizon shifts as we move our position, as we head closer or further away from our focal point.

Why is this important? The maturation and development of our perspectives requires us first to recognise that our prejudices *are there – as they are for others*. When we are attuned to our own prejudicial framework we become aware of how our perspective is provisional, historically contingent and changeable. But second, this openness to our own prejudices encourages a corresponding openness to transformative dialogue with different viewpoints. At the heart of Gadamerian hermeneutics is a notion of dialogue as 'the art of testing' (Gadamer 2004, p.360); we consider the potential truth in different perspectives and ways of understanding which fundamentally challenge our own prejudices. Consider how the common law functions, for example where precedent and previous judgments form the interpretive lens for legal advocates and judges. Yet the particulars of the case or changing norms in society can challenge or 'test' well-established interpretations of this preceding legal tradition.

Dialogue involves encountering something that is different and separate from ourselves (like another person, another cultural tradition, conceptual scheme or value framework), engaging with, working through and challenging our prejudices, with the intent of enriching our understanding. For example, I might have a prejudice about persons with schizophrenia being somehow 'dangerous', absorbed through social messaging, media stories and superficial observations of the man walking his dog in the park. When I encounter the man in the park, scared and presuming his dangerousness, I am actually faced with the reality that my frame of reference cannot make sense of this person and his behaviour in the first instance. But perhaps I actually talk to the man walking his dog and he explains how the hallucinations and voices help him cope with distress from various environmental triggers. Rather than hold fast to my prejudices, dialogue helps me realise the limits and flaws in the conceptual resources I have to understand something which seems foreign to me. I start to see this person with his own unique perspective; I cannot reduce him to some generalised stereotype, and the conversation has challenged my own long-held prejudices about persons with schizophrenia.

The aim of dialogue isn't to control or dominate another, nor to prove how one is right or passively accept our own limitations. Rather, dialogue involves the type of reciprocity involved in *asking* as well as *answering* questions. Gadamer writes:

> To someone who engages in dialogue only to prove himself right and not to gain insight, asking questions will indeed seem easier than answering them. There is no risk that he will be unable to answer a question. In fact, however, the continual failure of the interlocuter shows people who think they know better cannot even ask the right questions. In order to be able to ask, one must want to know, and that means knowing that one does not know. (Gadamer 2004, pp.356–357).

By asking and answering questions, we risk our own prejudices; we reveal and test our interpretive standpoint. This enables us to learn from others – whether this be their different manner of bodily coping in their environment, or their unique cognitive framework and value perspective, or their general way of experiencing the world.

Gadamer uses the image of a 'fusion of horizons' to help illustrate what happens when genuine understanding is achieved through dialogue. The image is slightly misleading because it seems to suggest that (1) our horizons are somehow completely separate in the first place; (2) genuine understanding denotes agreement or consensus. But in fact, what is a common human experience is this need to understand and be understood – this is in fact a 'common horizon' for us all. Equally, genuine understanding isn't reduced to consensus for Gadamer; indeed, a fusion of horizons is meant to describe how our encounter with something that seems foreign in the first instance evolves into one of many possibilities, where our understanding is improved and previous misunderstandings and distortions are corrected.

Gadamer's hermeneutics doesn't describe an objective, critical method, but a continually evolving process about refining and enriching our perspective through dialogue. It takes a great deal of effort and humility, but it also encourages us to face with honesty our unavoidable prejudices, values and perspectives. The encounter with the man walking his dog might not necessarily change all of your prejudices, but it should certainly help you eventually see him more as a *unique person* who deserves consideration the next time you see him in the park.

Further recommended reading

Benaroyo, Lazare and Widdershoven, Guy. (2004). 'Competence in mental health care: a hermeneutic approach.' *Health Care Analysis* 12: 295–306.

Gadamer, Hans-Georg. (1976). *Philosophical Hermeneutics*. Ed. and Trans. David E. Linge. Berkeley, CA: University of California.

Gadamer, Hans-Georg. (2004). *Truth and Method* (second edition). Trans. Joel Winsheimer and Donald G. Marshall. London: Continuum.

Svenaueus, Frederick. (2003). 'Hermeneutics of medicine in the wake of Gadamer: the issue of phronesis.' *Theoretical Medicine and Bioethics* 24: 407–431.

Taylor, Charles. (2011). 'Understanding the Other: A Gadamerian View of Conceptual Schemes.' In *Dilemmas and Connections*. Cambridge, MA: Harvard University Press.

Appendix 4: Duties of support

One of our arguments in this book has been that within certain constraints, practitioners can be justified in intervening in abusive, neglectful and coercive circumstances. The theoretical justification for this argument comes from two different angles. First is the feminist legal perspective on *relational rights,* which challenges the purported value neutrality and individualistic focus of legal rights and the law; second is the *Kantian argument for duties of assistance* which stems from the ideal of human agency and our limitations in achieving this ideal without the support of others.

Relational rights

Rights are often thought to apply mainly to *individuals,* where rights are essentially a property and entitlement of the individual. The right of autonomy, for example, is treated as a 'shield' to protect the individual from illegitimate outside interference, whether it be by the state or other individuals. A number of assumptions are implicit in this standard account of rights. First, individuals are seen as 'bounded' entities: a firm boundary exists between the self and others, and the boundary is enforced to protect the self from unwarranted outside intrusions. Second, the individual is abstract: the individual as rights holder is this abstract entity, removed from relationships, context and, indeed, the body. As such, the role of the law is to enforce respect for these rights and arbitrate any conflicts from an impartial perspective.

Feminist legal philosophers challenge this individualistic interpretation of rights, arguing that relationality often guides how rights are interpreted and enforced in the law. This relationality is evident, both in terms of the characteristics of individual rights-bearers and *how* the law actually functions in enforcing rights. Contrary to the picture of the rights holder as the 'bounded' self, relational approaches to rights argue that the boundary between self and others is fluid, embedded as we are within relationships of different kinds. Other individuals form part of ourselves depending on the relationship: a parent will see her child as part of her and her own good, just as a romantic partner is seen as an intrinsic part of oneself. Likewise, we are embodied selves, whose experiences involve the concrete realities of the body, emotion and perception, and of which themselves contain social and cultural meanings.

Fluid boundaries between self and other combined with the reality of embodiment mean that the actualisation, recognition and enforcement of rights will require varying levels of support and assistance. Much like the law has to respect and accommodate certain relevant bodily differences between men and women (such as when enforcing labour laws, making it illegal to discriminate women who may become pregnant or plan to have children), to respect the equal right of education for a person with a learning impairment will require a differential response to that of a person without. If we treated them the same (i.e., providing few accommodations or special needs teachers), this would in fact mean we are not treating the person with dyslexia equally. Sometimes to treat individuals equally it means we have to take differences into account. The point is that, this picture of the self as a bounded, abstract entity might help us tell a story about how to protect the individual from outside intrusion, but it says little about the types of supports and assistance that a person is entitled to once bodily difference and social context are taken into account.

Second, taking the embodied, socially embedded and relational self as our point of departure will also reveal a slightly different interpretation of what the law *does*: rather than simply act as a value-neutral vessel by which rules and rights can be enforced, it is itself imbued with certain values, and it implicitly structures and promotes certain relationships accordingly. A classic example is how the private–public divide is interpreted in the law. From a feminist legal perspective, the notion that the legal rights are simply there to protect one's private life from public interference is to ignore how this boundary itself makes a substantive statement about which power structures and relationships in the private sphere are tolerated. For example, if the law only prosecutes domestic abuse if the victim is willing to press charges, this communicates implicitly that relationships that are abusive, coercive and so on are tolerated in the private sphere, whereas the opposite is suggested in laws that prosecute abusers regardless of the victim's desire to press charges. Or whether the law sanctions same-sex marriage or recognises unmarried common-law partnerships tells us which types of relationships deserve protection and entitlements and, at a deeper level, are desirable and valuable.

Both of these points indicate that the law and its enforcement and recognition of rights are not value neutral, nor apply to individuals conceived as bounded selves. On these grounds, feminist jurists argue that rights need to be conceived along relational lines, so that our distinction between the private and public – or the sphere of non-interference and legitimate interference – will be much more fluid and open to negotiation, especially once we consider its differential impact on women as opposed to men, those with impairments as opposed to those without. From this perspective, interventions into so-called private relationships can be justified, particularly if a person's agency is seriously at risk (such as in cases of abuse). Indeed, if we are to treat such individuals *equally*, such interventions may be necessary. There is a recognition that failure to protect can emerge, both in the absence of positive supports and assistance and in failing to intervene within certain limits, in obvious cases of abuse and mistreatment. And recognising the relationality that runs through the law and its enforcement of rights means that we engage directly with the reasons for certain interventions and openly debate what constraints are appropriate.

Kantian duties of assistance

The philosophy of Immanuel Kant provides principled grounding for answering questions around whether third parties can be justified in intervening in abusive, neglectful or coercive relationships. This book draws inspiration from the implications of Kant's Formula of Humanity to justify and clarify the scope for third-party interventions. In the *Groundwork of the Metaphysic of Morals*, the Formula of Humanity enjoins that you 'Act in such a way that you always treat humanity, whether in your own person or in the person of any other, never simply as a means, but always at the same time as an end' (Kant 1948: 429[66–67]). Whereas 'things' have mere instrumental value (e.g., tools that we manipulate for our purposes, such as a hammer to help drive in a nail), humans are viewed as 'ends in themselves' and 'object[s] of reverence' (Kant 1948: 428[65]).

On a very superficial reading of the Formula, it provides an attractive, intuitive picture about the respect owed to persons due to her intrinsic dignity and value (and indeed, this is a connection that is often made in contemporary human rights literature). But problems emerge if we focus too closely on this aspect of dignity in Kant's philosophy, mainly because its highly demanding and moralised criteria potentially exclude all sorts of individuals (not just those with impairments).

Instead, the Formula of Humanity contains two crucial observations about human beings: (1) humans are unavoidably interdependent, embodied and imperfectly rational beings. We cannot actually assert, assume or act on the assumption that we as individuals are self-sufficient, given the premise of human interdependence and rational contingency. (2) Despite our imperfect, limited abilities, we nonetheless strive towards a kind of autonomous, temporally extended agency (namely, we structure our lives over an extended period of time through purposive goals and action). These two observations, in other words, describe a gap between our aspiration and abilities.

This gap between aspiration and abilities is bridged through a range of *negative* and *positive duties*.[1] Negative duties are where our actions and intentions are *constrained* or *impermissible*. Recognising others as end-setting agents as demanded by the Formula of Humanity sets constraints on *how* we treat others: the Formula implies negative duties where coercion or deception of other individuals is impermissible, because it involves treating others as mere means or tools to further our own goals, rather than as agents in their own right. When we purposively deceive someone or manipulate others for our own purposes, they are unable to genuinely assent or dissent.[2] By contrast, positive duties describe those duties and actions where we are required to act: recognising persons as end-setting agents in accordance with the Formula of Humanity means we are required to help and assist others to fulfil their own goal and ends. The fact that we struggle to realise our temporally extended agency through our own individual efforts means we all have an obligation to help and assist others, to facilitate and enable their agency. This means promoting the conditions through which our temporally extended agency can develop and flourish within ourselves and others.

These negative and positive duties together capture our obligations of beneficence towards others. Beneficence in the Kantian sense doesn't have the paternalistic overtones in our common definition in the medico-juridical context ('do no harm' or best interests), but rather, involves the active promotion of the ends of others, to cultivate a 'community of mutual aid' where the *conditions* of another's agency can be facilitated through support

---

1   Importantly, our account here is much more Kantian 'in spirit' than a strict exegesis of his philosophy. The metaphysics around Kant's moral philosophy cannot be easily dismissed, particularly in the context of liberal political philosophy, and there is an overwhelming tendency to dismiss his metaphysics arbitrarily. However, in the context of our book (and indeed in Kong 2017) the point is to explain how the dual assumptions about limited ability and aspiration capture an important dynamic within impairment and disability, and the role of assistance and support. We are not so committed to a Kantian framework and all his assumptions but recognise something intuitive about his articulation of this central tension in human agency.

2   This view sounds abstract, but actually resonates with the criteria for interventions based on the court's use of inherent jurisdiction.

and assistance. We encourage the autonomy skills of others and help them implement plans towards their own happiness. Any impulse to perfect or act for them would fundamentally disrespect a person as an end-setting agent and arrogantly ignores our own imperfection and rational contingency. Duties of assistance must be fulfilled with humility, refraining from manipulative, deceptive and arrogant impulses and behaving with generosity, gratitude, sympathy and compassion (Kant 1996, 6:386; 462–468; 453–461).

Both feminist and Kantian lines of argument provide philosophical justification for when interventions in disabling, abusive and neglectful relationships may be warranted. We tend to think of autonomous agency and beneficence as opposite sides of a scale. But as these different argumentative strands show, duties of assistance are part and parcel of recognising the substantive equality and rights of individuals, of taking seriously the relationality of selves, of realising a vision of ourselves as end-setting agents that can determine our lives in meaningful ways in light of our rational imperfection. The community of mutual aid and assistance includes us all, whether or not we have impairments.

Further recommended reading

Eldergill, Anselm. (2015). 'Compassion and the law: a judicial perspective.' *Elder Law Journal* 3:268–278.

Herman, Barbara. (1996). *The Practice of Moral Judgment.* Cambridge, MA: Harvard University Press.

Hill, Jr. Thomas E. (1991). *Autonomy and Self-Respect.* Cambridge: Cambridge University Press.

Kant, Immanuel. (1948). *Groundwork of the Metaphysics of Morals.* Trans. H.J. Paton. London: Routledge.

Kant, Immanuel. (1996). *The Metaphysics of Morals.* Trans. Mary Gregor. Cambridge: Cambridge University Press.

Lacey, Nicola. (1998). *Unspeakable Subjects: Feminist Essays in Legal and Social Theory.* Oxford: Hart.

Nedelsky, Jennifer. (2013). *Law's Relations: A Relational Theory of Self, Autonomy, and Law.* New York and Oxford: Oxford University Press.

O'Neill, Onora. (1985). 'Between consenting adults.' *Philosophy and Public Affairs* 14: 252–277.

Appendix 5: Practical resources

As we noted in Chapter 1, this is not a legal textbook in a conventional sense, a guide as to how to conduct a capacity or best interests assessment, or a guide as to how to conduct a safeguarding investigation under the Care Act 2014 or Social Services and Well-being (Wales) Act 2014. Rather, it is a guide to how to think about mental capacity in situations of complexity. To that end, it deliberately does not go in detail into all the intricacies of the overlapping legal frameworks that may be relevant in any given situation.

In this appendix, we set out useful resources for those who do need to navigate the complexities of the law in this area. We have deliberately sought to set out those resources which are either free or affordable (legal textbooks can be notoriously expensive).

Mental capacity

The background to and a detailed explanation of the MCA from a legal perspective can be found in Gordon Ashton (ed.), *Mental Capacity Law and Practice* (fourth edition, Jordan Publishing, 2018). Perhaps the best guide to the MCA from the perspective of social and healthcare professionals can be found in Matthew Graham and Jakki Cowley, *A Practical Guide to the Mental Capacity Act 2005: Putting the Principles of the Act Into Practice* (Jessica Kingsley Publishers, 2015). The subject of capacity assessment is addressed in detail in Alex Ruck Keene (general editor), *Assessment of Mental Capacity: A Practical Guide for Doctors and Lawyers* (fourth edition, British Medical Association and Law Society, 2015b). A very useful (free) resource on supporting individuals with impaired capacity to make financial decisions was produced by Empowerment Matters in 2014, entitled *Making Financial Decisions: Guidance for Assessing, Supporting and Empowering Specific Decision Making*, available at https://empowermentmattersweb.files.wordpress.com/2014/09/assessing-capacity-financial-decisions-guidance-final.pdf.

Maintained by 39 Essex Chambers, an extensive website of resources is dedicated to the MCA and includes case summaries and guides to both capacity and best interests assessment. There is also a (free) monthly Mental Capacity Report, which can be subscribed to at the same website: www.39essex.com/resources-and-training/mental-capacity-law. This is probably the easiest way in which to keep abreast of developments in this area, which continue to come thick and fast.

The practices and procedures of the Court of Protection are covered in a number of books, the most accessible being Alex Ruck Keene (ed.), *Court of Protection Handbook* (revised second edition, Legal Action Group, 2017), which is accompanied by a (free) website: www.courtofprotectionhandbook.com.

The website www.mentalhealthlawonline.co.uk is an extensive site containing legislation, case transcripts and other useful material relating to both the Mental Capacity Act 2005 and Mental Health Act 1983. The site also features a helpful (moderated) discussion list for professionals working in the area.

The Social Care Institute for Excellence maintains a useful database of mental capacity resources: www.scie.org.uk/mca-directory.

Safeguarding

The law in this area is subtly but importantly different across England and Wales, the Care Act 2014 applying in England, and the Social Services and Well-being (Wales) Act 2014. Adi Cooper OBE and Emily White (eds), *Safeguarding Adults Under the Care Act 2014* (Jessica Kingsley Publishers, 2017) is perhaps the best guide to adult safeguarding in England. Its core principles are equally applicable in Wales.

Community care

Issues relating to mental capacity and safeguarding frequently rub up against the provision of community care services. This is particularly so where decisions made by local authorities (or NHS bodies in the case of continuing healthcare) set the 'available options' between which choices have to be made on the part of the individual with impaired capacity. The law in this area was clarified by the Supreme Court in *N v ACCG* [2017] UKSC 22, which is summarised and commented on at: www.39essex.com/cop_cases/ n-v-accg. A reliable guide to the complexities of community care law more broadly is Luke Clements, *Community Care and the Law* (sixth edition, Legal Action Group, 2017). This does not cover Wales, but *Rhydian*, a website maintained by Ann James and Luke Clements, provides an overview and critical commentary: www. lukeclements.co.uk/rhydian-social-welfare-law-in-wales.

References and Further Information

Bibliography

Agich, George. (1993). *Autonomy and Long-Term Care*. New York, NY; Oxford: Oxford University Press.

Arvidsson, Patrik, Granlund, Mats, and Thyberg, Mikael. (2008). 'Factors related to self-rated participation in adolescents and adults with mild intellectual disability – a systematic literature review.' *Journal of Applied Research in Intellectual Disabilities* 21(3): 277–291.

Ashton, Gordon, Marin, Marc, van Overdijk, Claire, Ruck Keene, Alex, Terrell, Martin, and Ward, Adrian D. (2018). *Mental Capacity Law and Practice* (fourth edition). Bristol: Jordan Publishing.

Bach, Michael and Kerzner, Lana. (2010). *A New Paradigm for Protecting Autonomy and the Right to Legal Capacity*. Ontario: Law Commission of Ontario.

Benaroyo, Lazare and Widdershoven, Guy. (2004). 'Competence in mental health care: a hermeneutic approach.' *Health Care Analysis* 12: 295–306.

Benson, Paul. (1994). 'Free agency and self-worth.' *Journal of Philosophy* 91: 650–668.

Charland, Louis. (1998). 'Is Mr. Spock mentally competent?' *Philosophy, Psychiatry and Psychology*, 5(1): 67–86.

Clements, Luke. (2017). *Community Care and the Law* (second edition). London: Legal Action Group.

Cooper, Adi and White, Emily. (2017). *Safeguarding Adults Under the Care Act 2014*. London: Jessica Kingsley Publishers.

Crown Prosecution Service. (September 2012). 'CPS Policy for Prosecuting Cases of Rape.' Accessed on 13/06/2018 at: www.cps.gov.uk/publication/cps-policy-prosecuting-cases-rape.

Dreyfus, Hubert. L. (2014). *Skillful Coping: Essays on the Phenomenology of Everyday Perception and Action*. Oxford: Oxford University Press.

Dworkin, Gerald. (1976). 'Autonomy and behavior control.' *Hastings Center Report* 6: 23–28.

Eldergill, Anselm. (2015). 'Compassion and the law: a judicial perspective.' *Elder Law Journal* 3: 268–278.

Foley, Kitty-Rose, Jacoby, Peter, Einfeld, Stewart, Girdler, Sonja, *et al*. (2014). 'Day occupation is associated with psychopathology for adolescents and young adults with Down syndrome'. *BMC Psychiatry* 14: 266.

Frankfurt, Harry. (1971). 'Freedom of the will and the concept of a person.' *Journal of Philosophy* 68: 5–20.

Gadamer, Hans-Georg. (1976). *Philosophical Hermeneutics.* Ed. and Trans. David E. Linge. Berkeley, CA: University of California.

Gadamer, Hans-Georg. (2004). *Truth and Method* (second edition). Trans. Joel Winsheimer and Donald G. Marshall. London: Continuum.

Goffman, E. (1963). *Stigma: Notes on the Management of Spoiled Identity.* Englewood Cliffs, NJ: Prentice-Hall.

Graham, Matthew and Cowley, Jakki. (2015). *A Practical Guide to the Mental Capacity Act 2005: Putting the Principles of the Act into Practice.* London: Jessica Kingsley Publishers.

Green, Sara, Davis, Christine, Karshmer, Elana, Marsh, Pete, and Straight, Benjamin. (2005). 'Living stigma: the impact of labeling, stereotyping, separation, status loss, and discrimination in the lives of individuals with disabilities and their families.' *Sociological Inquiry* 75(2): 197–215.

Hedley, Sir Mark. (2016). *Modern Judge: Power, Responsibility and Society's Expectations.* Bristol: Jordan Publishing.

Hegel, Georg Wilhelm Friedrich. (1977). *Phenomenology of Spirit.* Trans. A.V. Miller. Oxford: Clarendon Press.

Herman, Barbara. (1996). *The Practice of Moral Judgment.* Cambridge, MA: Harvard University Press.

Hill, Jr. Thomas E. (1991). *Autonomy and Self-Respect.* Cambridge: Cambridge University Press.

House of Lords Select Committee. (2014). *Mental Capacity Act 2005: Post-Legislative Scrutiny.* London: The Stationery Office.

Jahoda, Andrew, Wilson, Alastair, Stalker, Kirsten, and Cairney, Anja. (2010). 'Living with stigma and the self-perceptions of people with mild intellectual disabilities.' *Journal of Social Issues* 66(3): 521–534.

Kant, Immanuel. (1948). *Groundwork of the Metaphysic of Morals.* Trans. H.J. Paton. London: Routledge.

Kant, Immanuel. (1996). *The Metaphysics of Morals.* Trans. Mary Gregor. Cambridge: Cambridge University Press.

Kittay, Eva Feder. (2005). 'At the margins of personhood.' *Ethics* 116: 100–131.

Kittay, Eva Feder. (1999). *Love's Labor: Essays on Women, Equality, and Dependency.* New York, NY: Routledge.

Kong, Camillia. (2014). 'Beyond the balancing scales: the importance of prejudice and dialogue in *A Local Authority v E and Others.*' *Child and Family Law Quarterly* 26: 216–236.

Kong, Camillia. (2017). *Mental Capacity in Relationship: Decision-Making, Dialogue, and Autonomy.* Cambridge: Cambridge University Press.

Lacey, Nicola. (1998). *Unspeakable Subjects: Feminist Essays in Legal and Social Theory.* Oxford: Hart.

Law Commission. (2017). *Mental Capacity and Deprivation of Liberty* (Law Comm No 372). London: The Stationery Office.

Lindemann Nelson, Hilde. (2001). *Damaged Identities; Narrative Repair*. Ithaca, NY: Cornell University Press.

Mackenzie, Catriona and Stoljar, Natalie. (eds) (2000*). Relational Autonomy: Feminist Perspectives on Autonomy, Agency, and the Social Self*. New York, NY: Oxford University Press.

McMahan, Jeff. (2003). *The Ethics of Killing: Problems at the Margins of Life*. New York, NY: Oxford University Press.

Meyers, Diana T. (1989). *Self, Society, and Personal Choice*. New York, NY: Columbia University Press.

Naoki, Higashida. (2007). *The Reason I Jump*. Trans. K.A. Yoshida and David Mitchell. London: Sceptre.

Neary, Mark. (2017, 27 September). #MCA10 D is for Dad [Blog post]. *Adult Principal Social Worker Network*. Available at: https://adultpswnetwork. wordpress.com/2017/09/27/mca10-d-is-for-dad-guest-blog-from-mark-neary.

Nedelsky, Jennifer. (2013). *Law's Relations: A Relational Theory of Self, Autonomy, and Law*. New York and Oxford: Oxford University Press.

Oliver, Michael. (2009). *Understanding Disability: From Theory to Practice* (second edition). Basingstoke; New York, NY: Palgrave Macmillan.

O'Neill, Onora. (1985). 'Between consenting adults.' *Philosophy and Public Affairs* 14: 252–277.

Quinn, Gerard. (2010, February). 'Personhood & Legal Capacity: Perspectives on the Paradigm Shift of Article 12 CRPD.' Conference on Disability and Legal Capacity under the CRPD. Harvard Law School, Boston (Vol. 20, pp.3–5).

Ruck Keene, Alex. (2015a). 'Capacity is not an off-switch.' Mental Capacity Law and Policy. Accessed on 13/06/2018 at: www.mentalcapacitylawandpolicy. org.uk/capacity-is-not-an-off-switch.

Ruck Keene, Alex. (2015b). *Assessment of Mental Capacity: A Practical Guide for Doctors and Lawyers* (fourth edition). London: British Medical Association and the Law Society.

Ruck Keene, Alex. (2017). *Court of Protection Handbook* (revised second edition). London: Legal Action Group.

Ruck Keene, Alex, and Auckland, Cressida. (2015). 'More presumptions please? wishes, feelings and best interests decision-making'. *Elder Law Journal* 5(3) 293–301.

Shakespeare, Tom. (2006). *Disability Rights and Wrongs*. London: Routledge.

Svenaueus, Frederick. (2003). 'Hermeneutics of medicine in the wake of Gadamer: the issue of phronesis.' *Theoretical Medicine and Bioethics* 24: 407–431.

Tan, Jacinta, Hope, Tony, and Stewart, Anne. (2003). 'Competence to refuse treatment in anorexia nervosa.' *International Journal of Law and Psychiatry* 26: 697–707.

Taylor, Charles. (2011). 'Understanding the Other: A Gadamerian View of Conceptual Schemes.' In *Dilemmas and Connections*. Cambridge, MA: Harvard University Press.
United Nations Committee on the Rights of Persons with Disabilities. (April 2014). *General Comment No. 1 – Article 12: Equal Recognition Before the Law* (CRPD/C/GC/1).
United Nations Commission for the Protection of Rights of Persons with Disabilities. (2017). *Concluding observations on the initial report of the United Kingdom of Great Britain and Northern Ireland* (CRPD/C/GBR/CO/1).
Ward, Adrian. (2003). *Adult Incapacity Legislation*. Edinburgh: W. Green.
WHO (World Health Organization). (2002). *Toward a Common Language for Functioning, Disability, and Health, ICF*. Geneva: WHO.

Statutes

Care Act 2014

Mental Capacity Act 2005

Social Services and Well-being (Wales) Act 2014

International instruments

European Convention on Human Rights

United Nations Convention on the Rights of Persons with Disabilities

Cases (England & Wales)

Aintree University Hospitals NHS Foundation Trust v James [2013] UKSC 67

A Local Authority v (1) MA (2) NA and (3) SA [2005] EWHC 2942

A Local Authority v WMA & MA [2013] EWCOP 50

Briggs v Briggs & Ors [2016] EWCOP 53

DL v A Local Authority and Others [2012] EWCA Civ 253

King's College NHS Trust v C & V [2015] EWCOP 80

LBX v K & Ors [2013] EWHC 3230 (Fam) and [2013] EWHC 4170 (Fam)

The London Borough of Redbridge v G and Others [2014] EWHC 485 (COP)

N v ACCG [2017] UKSC 22

NCC v TB and PB [2014] EWCOP 14

Re A (Capacity: Refusal of Contraception) [2010] EWHC 1549 (Fam)

Re ITW [2009] EWHC 2525 (Fam)

Re ML [2014] EWCOP 2

Re MM (an adult) [2007] EWHC 2003 (Fam)

Re MP; LBH v GP [2009] Claim No: FD08P01058

PC & NC v City of York Council [2013] EWCA Civ 478

Westminster City Council v Sykes [2014] EWCOP B9

Wye Valley NHS Trust v B [2015] EWCOP 60

Cases (international)

Re BKR [2015] SGCA 26

Index